How Now Shall We Live?

Student Edition Leader's Guide

Charles Colson
and Nancy Pearcey

with Small Group Activities by
Ann Cannon

LifeWay Press
Nashville, Tennessee

ISBN 0-6330-0450-2

Dewey Decimal Classification: 248.83
Subject Headings: CHRISTIAN LIFE, TEENAGERS, SALVATION

The book *How Now Shall We Live? Student Edition* is the text for course CG-0569
in the study area Personal Life-Youth in the Christian Growth Study Plan.

Unless otherwise noted, Scripture quotations are from the Holy Bible,
New International Version, copyright © 1973, 1978, 1984
by International Bible Society.

Order additional copies of this book by writing to Customer Service Center, MSN 113;
127 Ninth Avenue, North; Nashville, TN 37234-0113; by calling toll free (800) 458-2772;
by faxing (615) 251-5933; by ordering online at www.lifeway.com; by emailing
customerservice@lifeway.com; or by visiting a LifeWay Christian Store.

Youth Section
Discipleship and Family Group
LifeWay Christian Resources
of the Southern Baptist Convention

Printed in the United States of America

LifeWay Press
127 Ninth Avenue, North
Nashville, Tennessee 37234-0152

As God works through us, we will help people and churches know Jesus Christ and seek His king-
dom by providing biblical solutions that spiritually transform individuals and cultures.

Contents

Introduction

21st Century Students

Here's a checklist of today's generation:

- ❑ They believe in moral relativism—whatever feels right, is.
- ❑ They refuse to obey authorities.
- ❑ Family is based on acceptance, not birth.
- ❑ They live in a world of virtual reality—what feels real in experience may not be real in fact.
- ❑ They see the world growing worse, as they live with news of Bosnia, Kosovo, AIDS, and wars fought in their neighborhoods and on their school campuses.
- ❑ They have a deep spiritual hunger, which is not necessarily Christian. In fact, they mix and match theologies, values, and ideas.
- ❑ Many in this generation know nothing about the Bible, Christianity, or that Jesus Christ is more than a cuss word.
- ❑ They hesitate to trust others because they are not trustworthy themselves.
- ❑ They live for the moment with no thought of the future.

These are the students you are trying to interest in an eight-week commitment of extra study, difficult topics, and heavy-duty concepts. Your task is neither easy, nor enviable.

Would I do it? Even for one student!

Why? Because that student can change the world. I've seen them do it.

This is also today's generation:

- ❑ They started See You at the Pole, a movement on campuses across America that continues to grow. I know one freshman who heard about See You at the Pole from her youth minister, talked to her school principal, and prayed with three students at the flag pole the first year. This year there were 300.
- ❑ They accepted the challenge that they didn't have to have sex before marriage. Through their commitments they have made True Love Waits and sexual abstinence until marriage a major, worldwide trend.
- ❑ They connect in technical ways we never dreamed of. They unite in prayer using beepers and cell phones. They witness to other students in chat rooms. They use the Internet to find tangible help for hurting friends.
- ❑ They seek out tough service projects, flocking to sweat-oriented summer camps like World Changers and M-Fuge, and actively work alongside adults to build Habitat for Humanity homes.

Making It Work

Consider these ideas as you plan and prepare.

- ❑ Personally invite each student. Look for students who want to grow spiritually, who show an interest in biblical ideas, who are stepping up to leadership positions, who want to help others. Don't forget, however, the quiet student who may not speak up in a class setting, but works hard on service projects.
- ❑ Select an informal setting away from your church. Consider a home, a general purpose room in an apartment complex or in a campus dormitory (get permission), or a community center located near your students. At the Introductory Session you can discuss where to meet on a regular basis.
- ❑ Select a time when students can come. Don't think of Sundays or Wednesdays only. How about Thursday nights, Saturday afternoons, or Tuesdays before school? Don't think 7 p.m. only. Consider 5:30 p.m. with a snack supper. Or, 7 a.m. with a fast food breakfast. What about early afternoon for students on split sessions?
- ❑ Purchase the *How Now Shall We Live? Student Edition Video* (ISBN 0-6330-3530-0). This 120-minute videotape is essential to the study. There are eight segments, one for each unit of study. Each segment contains a humorous, yet direct, look at that week's topics plus a personal interview with Charles Colson sharing his passion and commitment. This professionally produced video is only $39.95 and can be purchased at Lifeway Christian Stores or any Christian bookstore, or by calling Lifeway at 1-800-458-2772.
- ❑ Look through the *How Now Shall We Live? Student Edition*. The material is weighty. Younger students may not understand the abstract ideas or the relevancy. But there are also powerful stories, incredible insights, and supportive Bible studies. The challenge will be to persuade students to hang in there through a couple of weeks of difficult study. The payoff at the end, however, is terrific. Warning: You cannot pick up this material two hours before the group session and lead your students with integrity and understanding.
- ❑ Show your students the made-for-TV movie, *Katy's Metaphysical Adventure*, which is found in the adult's *How Now Shall We Live? Leader Kit* (ISBN 0-6330-3530-0). Show this movie at your introductory session, or use it as a promotional piece before your study begins.

Those of us who worked on this material pray that the results of our work and prayers will be students ready to claim their culture for Christ. We believe it can happen!

Introductory Session

Session Goals

This session is designed to help students:
- understand what the eight-week study involves;
- evaluate their need for the study;
- make a commitment to become involved.

Before the Session

- ❏ Get *How Now Shall We Live? Student Edition* books.
- ❏ Duplicate Worksheets 1 "I Believe" and 17 "Treasure Hunt."
- ❏ Purchase chocolate candy that comes in nuggets.
- ❏ Cut apart each item on Worksheet 17, wrap it around a chocolate candy nugget, and hide these in the meeting room.

During the Session

GETTING INVOLVED (15 minutes)
Step 1—Questions
Start with these basic questions. Ask:
- **What do you do or say when your science teacher talks about evolution?**
- **How do you responds when friends ask about your faith?**
- **How do your beliefs affect other areas of your life?**
- **Do you know why you believe what you believe?**

Tell Becky's story. Becky and another student in her science class disagreed about evolution. She tried to score points by using her Bible and arguing her faith. She got nowhere. After talking with her youth minister, Becky changed her tactics. "I've decided to listen to what you have to say," Becky told the guy. "I can learn from you, and maybe you can learn from me." Their arguments settled into thoughtful discussions that intrigued the whole class. Becky didn't like everything she heard, but she saw how studying the other side helped her present a more believable case for creation. Becky's story is what this eight-week study is about—knowing what you believe, seeing what others believe, and finding out how to make a difference. Hand out Worksheet 1 "I Believe." Tell students to mark their selections. Let volunteers share. Explain that students will see this sheet in the final unit, where they may notice changes in their opinions.

FOCUSING ON THE FACTS (25 minutes)
Step 2—Purpose
Display a large sheet of paper on which you've written this purpose: Our task is to produce students who un-derstand the ideas that are building and destroying our world so that Christian students can be salt and light to this generation. State that our culture is divided into two major systems that are exactly opposite. Hand out copies of *How Now Shall We Live? Student Edition.* Direct two students to turn to page 16, with one reading the paragraph beginning "Naturalism is the idea. . ." and the other reading the paragraph "By contrast, Christianity. . ." Explain who Charles Colson is. State that the study is divided into eight weeks. Call on different student to read aloud each unit's opening page. Those pages are 9, 29, 53, 72, 90, 109, 134, and 153.

Tell students they now have a chance to check out the material for themselves in a treasure hunt. Tell them that you hid 24 "nuggets" of information around the room. They can hunt for as many nuggets as they want, but they need to be prepared to share their "treasures" with everyone. Let students look for the nuggets hidden in the room. Call for students to share their information, not their chocolate nuggets.

MAKING IT REAL (10 minutes)
Step 3—Tough It Out!
Honestly discuss what's involved in this study—a 30-minute a day commitment, five days a week plus a group session once a week. Let students know the study involves theories and philosophies that may be new and difficult, while other ideas will be more familiar. Explain that the weekly group sessions offer ways to review the material and sort out the more confusing ideas.

Read the final paragraph on page 7 (continued on page 8) of the Student Edition. Ask:
- **What do you think a "springtime" for Christianity means?**
- **Can students really make a difference?**

LEAVING PREPARED (10 minutes)
Step 4—The Practical Stuff
Discuss when to meet (day and time), where to meet, and the need for communication and encouragement during the week. Get e-mail addresses and phone numbers. Assign prayer partners, if possible. Share your encouragement and excitement for the project. Answer questions.

Suggest students write a statement of commitment in the front part of their the Student Editions. Pray for students as they begin this first week of study.

UNIT ONE

How We See Our World

Session Goals
This session is designed to help students:
• define and understand the concept of worldview;
• grasp the importance of ideas;
• begin to evaluate ideas in the remaining weeks of study.

Session Overview
Step 1: The Story of Jorge Crespo—Evaluate this story of dedication and determination.
Step 2: To Tell the Truth—Discover several worldviews.
Step 3: Three Key Questions—Determine how different theories answer the three worldview questions.
Step 4: Concentrate—Understand key words and how they relate to a person's worldview.
Step 5: Shifting Sands—Begin to identify a personal worldview.

Before the Session
GATHER:
❑ extra copies of *How Now Shall We Live? Student Edition* for visitors or new participants
❑ extra Bibles for visual support
❑ Bring the "Purpose" statement from the introductory session for use in Step 3.

for Step 2
❑ *How Now Shall We Live? Student Edition Video*
❑ TV-VCR
❑ a large sheet of paper, marker

for Step 3
❑ table salt or rock salt

for Step 4
❑ small prizes for winning team (gum, lollipops, coupons)

for Step 5
❑ a small, flat stone for each student
❑ permanent markers

DO:
for visual support
❑ Write the three worldview questions from page 12 of the *Student Edition* on a large sheet of paper.

for Step 1
❑ Enlist a student to review and summarize the story of Jorge Crespo on page 10 of the *Student Edition*.

for Step 2
❑ Duplicate Worksheet 2, "Tell the Truth" cards. Cut the cards apart to give one card to each reader.

for Step 4
❑ Duplicate Worksheets 3A and 3B, "Concentration Game" onto one page. Make more than one copy of the game if you have a large group and will be playing two or more games at the same time. Cut along the dotted lines, stacking them numbered side up.

During the Session

GETTING INVOLVED (5 minutes)
Step 1: The Story of Jorge Crespo
Before the session, enlist one student to review and summarize the story of Jorge Crespo in "A Journey from Hell to Heaven," page 10 in *How Now Shall We Live? Student Edition*.

Begin the session by asking the enlisted student to tell the story. Ask:
• **How did you feel the first time you read Crespo's story?**
• **How does hearing it again make you feel?**
• **Why would someone do all that for prisoners?**
• **What might be Crespo's worldview?**
• **Why do you think Charles Colson told this story at the beginning of his book *How Now Shall We Live?***

Say: **Most students today don't know what a worldview is. Jorge Crespo's story gives us a dramatic picture of two contrasting worldviews. Understanding the idea of worldview was your assignment this week. Let's see how you did.**

FOCUSING ON THE FACTS (35 minutes)
Step 2: Tell the Truth
This is the copy of Worksheet 2, "Tell the Truth":

Card #1—I am Professor Anne Arkist—a scientist and a zoologist. In fact, I am President of the International Society for People With More Brains Than They Need—oh, yes, and the mother of two. I believe that evil is merely bad behavior resulting from the repressive, closed-minded, male dominated, Judeo-Christian culture.

Card #2—I am a renowned psychologist from Kahuna Luna's Center for Meditative Oneness in Laguna Beach. I've written over a half-dozen pamphlets on living with bad karma. I enjoy surfing and barnacle harvesting. You can call me Monty. I believe that truth cannot be defined or measured, but is real only if I think it is real.

Card #3—I am a salesman with an answer for every possible question you might have. I can guarantee that my answers will calm every teenage anxiety, fill every student's heart, and soothe every youthful problem. No more wondering about where you came from or why you're here. My product—Naturalism—says "Build your own life! Forget about an afterlife. Who needs it? You've got today, so make the most of it."

Ask for three volunteers. Give each volunteer a card. Tell the others to determine which person is expressing a worldview based on truth. After the cards have been read, ask: **Which one is expressing a worldview based on truth?** (Actually, none.) Challenge students to support their answers.

Say: **Watch this video to see what a worldview is, and how the ideas of these three people fit in.**

Play the first segment of the *How Now Shall We Live? Student Edition Video*, through the interview with Charles Colson.

Ask: **Based on Charles Colson's definition and what you studied this week, how would you define worldview?**
Write the students' definition on a large sheet of paper.

Step 3: Three Key Questions
Before the session, write the three questions of a worldview from page 12 in the Student Edition on a large poster. Display this poster. Divide students into two teams. Direct one team to decide how someone with a Christian worldview would answer these questions. Tell the other team to decide how someone with a naturalistic worldview would answer the questions. Encourage both teams to use their books, especially the information in Day Two. Call on each team to present its answers to the questions.

Review the "Purpose" visual from the introductory session. Direct students to underline *Matthew 5:13-14* in their Bibles as verses to memorize and use throughout the next seven weeks. Place a small amount of salt in each person's hand. Ask:
• **What is the purpose of salt?**
• **How does salt lose its saltiness?** (Not used, too much humidity, gets stale)
• **How are Christians the "salt of the earth"?**
• **How do some Christians lose their "saltiness"?** (Watering down their Christian worldview with other views is one example.)
• **How are Christians the "lights of the world"?**
• **How can this study help you become salt and light?**

ADDITIONALLY . . . 1
If you have more than an hour for this session, lead students to share their findings about wisdom. Assign each of the following Scripture references to four students to look-up: *1 Kings 3:28, Psalm 111:10, Proverbs 1:7,* and *Proverbs 9:10.* Direct students to page 20 in the Student Edition. After the first student reads *1 Kings 3:28*, call on volunteers to share their answers to number one (What is the source of wisdom?). Let the second student read *Psalms 111:10.* Invite students to share their answers to this question. Continue reading the Scripture and discussing it using the questions in the student book.

Turn to page 21. Ask three more students to read aloud *Proverbs 12:8; 24:14;* and *28:26.* After each verse invite volunteers to share their thoughts on wisdom.

ADDITIONALLY . . . 2
If you have more than an hour for this session, create a debate. Divide students into two teams. Let one team defend the statement and the other team refute the statement. The statement is: Ideas have consequences. Although the statement comes from Day Three, encourage teams to use the whole week's information in preparing their arguments. Use an informal debate format with one side presenting its arguments, followed by the other team. Invite each side to challenge the other team's points. Challenge students to support their ideas with Scripture (several passages are suggested in the Student Edition).

OPTION 1
Instead of a debate, involve students in a pro-con analysis of two different sentences from Unit One. Assign one team to look at the statement: Ideas have consequences. Direct another team to analyze the statement: The Christian calling is not only to save souls but to save minds. (Both come from p. 21 in the Student Edition.) After teams have developed several points, let them share with one another.

MAKING IT REAL (10 minutes)
Step 4: Concentrate
To confirm that students understand key words used in Unit One, play a game of Concentration. Duplicate Worksheet 3 (sides A and B). Cut apart the duplicated cards. Place the cards numbered side up on a table or the floor. Divide students into two teams. (With a large group, make two or more sets of cards and set up two or

more games in different corners of the meeting area.)

Say: **This week you saw words that may have been unfamiliar to you. Or, you may have heard the word before but didn't know it's meaning. To help you recall these words and their definitions, let's play Concentration. The objective is to match a word with it's definition.** Don't let students use their books.

First, one team turns over two cards, trying to make a match (a word and its definition). If they are unsuccessful the other team turns over two cards. The team with the most matches wins. Give the winning team small prizes (lollipops, gum, coupons for a soft drink at a fast food place). Here are the words and correct matches adapted from the Student Edition:

- **philosophy**—the most general beliefs, concepts, and attitudes of an individual or group.
- **naturalism**—the belief that scientific laws are adequate for all phenomena; denies that any event or object can have supernatural significance.
- **cultural commission**—the call to create a culture under the lordship of Christ.
- **theism**—the belief in God.
- **communism**—the belief that does away with private property through a system in which goods are owned in common and are available as needed.
- **pragmatism**—the belief that whatever works best is right.
- **enlightenment**—movement that rejected traditional social, religious, and political ideas to emphasize that reasoning decides right from wrong.
- **utopianism**—the belief that the right social and economic structures will create an age of harmony and prosperity.
- **postmodernism**—the belief that in life there is no right or wrong.
- **deconstructionism**—postmodern belief that law is based on the opinion of who is in power at the time.

After playing the game, say: **These words will be used in your studies over the next seven weeks. Understanding these words will help you identify other worldviews. It will also help you establish a Christian worldview.**

Lead students to decide which philosophies/theories are not Christian (naturalism, communism, pragmatism, enlightenment, utopianism, postmodernism, deconstructionism). If you work with older students, suggest they take each belief and find a Scripture that refutes that belief.

OPTION 2
Direct students to page 21 in the Student Edition. Ask:
- **What "skirmishes" did you draw on your tree?**
- **What roots did you write in as the roots of your tree?**

Point out that in the coming weeks students will see how to respond to these skirmishes.

ADDITIONALLY . . . 3
If you have more than one hour for this session, say: **In this first week Colson mentions that "the Christian faith cannot be reduced to John 3:16 or simple formulas." (p. 19)**
Ask: **Why is John 3:16 not enough for a Christian's worldview statement?**

LEAVING PREPARED (10 minutes)
Step 5: Shifting Sands
Ask a student to read *Matthew 7:24-26*. Direct students to turn to page 22 in the Student Edition. Call on volunteers to share where they placed God in their "houses."
Say: **You've studied the shifting sands of four men.** Assign four teams of students either Descartes, Rousseau, Darwin, or Nietzsche. Tell teams to summarize the philosophy of their assigned man. After students report, ask:
- **What shifting sands are these philosophies built on?**
- **How do these ideas relate to a Christian worldview?**

Direct students to page 25 in the Student Edition. Ask them to share responses to the question: Why do you suppose we humans cling so stubbornly to failed and false systems?

Challenge students to consider how they can use this information about different worldviews in their lives. Write their comments on a whiteboard. To help them get started, ask questions like these:
- **When you hear someone offer an opinion based on a false worldviews, how might you respond?**
- **How has this week's study made you sensitive to what others say and do?**
- **How would you share with a friend what you're studied this week?**
- **What do you want to know about another's worldview?**

Before leaving, ask students to write their own worldview statements. Suggest they write the statement in pencil on the inside front cover of the Student Edition. Then, as they continue to work through these weeks they can make changes to their worldview statement. Hand a small, flat stone and a permanent marker to each student. Read *Matthew 7:24-26* again. Tell students to find a Scripture either in their Bibles or from the verses listed in the Student Edition. Encourage them to write the Bible reference on the rock, and keep the rock as reminder of God being the solid foundation for Christians.

> **OPTION 3**
> As an alternate to this step, older students can discuss the closing statements from Day Five. In the next to the last paragraph on page 28 of the Student Edition, Colson writes, "When the church is truly the church, a community living in biblical obedience and contending for faith in every area of life, it will surely revive the surrounding culture, or create a new one." In the footnote related to that statement, notice this quote "The church exists merely for the sake of God." Ask students to evaluate what that last statement means. Then, lead students to describe how the church can revive an unhealthy culture or create a new one.

UNIT TWO
Chemicals, It's All Chemicals

Session Goals
This session is designed to help students:
• evaluate several scientific theories of creation;
• relate these theories to divine creation;
• focus on the evidence for divine creation.

Session Overview
Step 1: The Missing Piece—Use incomplete puzzles to explain what's missing in some scientific theories of creation.
Step 2: Research Sites—Examine key points in creation theories and compare these to divine creation.
Step 3: Questions, Anyone?—Discuss questions students have.
Step 4: Experience Creation—Go on a creation walk.
Step 5: Worship God—Use several ways to worship God.

Before the Session

GATHER:
❏ extra copies of *How Now Shall We Live? Student Edition* for visitors
❏ extra Bibles

for Step 1
❏ two sheets of poster board
❏ markers
❏ scissors

for Step 2
❏ pencils
❏ large sheets of paper
❏ markers

for Option 2
❏ personal computer with Internet hook-up

for Step 3
❏ *How Now Shall We Live? Student Edition Video*
❏ TV-VCR

for Additionally . . .1
❏ popcorn
❏ popcorn bags

for Step 4
❏ fruit (apples, grapes, strawberries, bananas) and/or vegetables (celery stalks, peeled carrots)
❏ bowl or basket for the fruit

DO:
for Step 1
❏ Make and cut apart the two puzzle posters. Remove one large piece from one puzzle.

for Option 1
❏ Invite a scientist who can communicate comfortably with students.

for Step 2
❏ Duplicate Worksheet 4 "Research Sites."

for Option 2
❏ Enlist someone to operate the computer.

for Step 3
❏ Duplicate Worksheet 5A "We've Got Questions"/5B "Doxology." Cut the copies apart. Save the copies of 5B for Step 5.

for Additionally . . . 1
❏ Bring small bags of popped popcorn.

During the Session

GETTING INVOLVED (10 minutes)
Step 1—The Missing Piece
Before the session, prepare two large puzzles using two different colors of poster board. On one poster

board randomly write the following theories in large letters, using different colored markers: *chemical reaction, cosmic ancestry, evolution, random mutation, natural selection, imaginary time, self-generation*. On the other poster board randomly write the following theories in large letters, using different colored markers: *big bang, anthropic principle, God's perfect design*. (Write this shorter number of theories two or three times on this poster.) Cut each poster into small- and medium-sized pieces to create a puzzle. Remove a crucial piece from the first puzzle (the one with *chemical reaction* written on it).

Place both puzzles on the floor. Direct arriving students to work together to assemble both puzzles. When students have completed the puzzles, ask:
• **What's wrong with one of the puzzles?**
• **How does the missing puzzle piece relate to the theories of creation you studied this week?**
• **What is that missing piece in each creation theory? (God)**

Say: **This week you studied information that probably made you feel like you were in a science class. But, it's important to understand these different theories and their faults so you can identify them when you see them in other places, such as in your schools.**

Invite students to share examples of what ideas were difficult to understand. Explain that they will have opportunities to ask their questions and get answers during this group session. Encourage them to remain faithful to their commitment to do this eight-week study.

OPTION 1
Instead of using Step 1, invite a scientist who is a Christian to speak to your students. Choose someone who communicates well with students, someone who avoids scientific jargon. Also, be sure you know this person's position on naturalistic theories. Suggest the person discuss the different evidences for divine creation presented in Unit Two. The person could show a DNA model or a cell model, for example. Allow time for students to ask questions. Invite the scientist to stay through the remainder of the session to answer questions as they come up.

FOCUSING ON THE FACTS (20 minutes)
Step 2—Research Sites
Hand out copies of Worksheet 4 "Research Sites" and pencils. Assign each student one day on the worksheet. If you have more than five students, let them work in pairs or small teams. Direct students to determine the main points from their assigned day. Suggest they also make notes about the Scripture suggested. Prompt students to add their own Scripture, as it comes to mind.

Next, challenge students to use a creative way to pre-

sent their information. Suggest that they either prepare a legal argument as a prosecutor, make up a skit to present one side and then the other, or write a rap or choral reading with made-up sign language. Be prepared to offer suggestions, but try to let students do their own study and work. If they are working with another person or in teams, encourage students to compare notes on their assigned day. Provide large sheets of paper and markers for the rap or choral reading creators. Call for each person's (team's) results. Ask:
• **Each time you read or heard evidence of divine creation, how did that make you feel?**
• **How willing would a non-Christian friend be to listen to this evidence?**
• **What other theories about creation have you studied in school or heard about?**
• **How would the evidence in this unit help you refute these other theories?**

OPTION 2
If you have Internet access and a personal computer, use a search machine (Yahoo, Excite, Alta Vista) to research creation. Type in *creation, evolution, big bang theory,* and other related words. Both Christian and secular sites offer persuasive arguments. Lead students to evaluate these points using the information they've learned this week. A couple of websites are mentioned in the Student Edition on page 34. If you use this option, visit several websites prior to the session. Be aware of the information on websites. If you don't have a computer and Internet hook-up at home, but will be using this option during the session (thanks to another's expertise), visit your local library. Most libraries have Internet access.

MAKING IT REAL (25 minutes)
Step 3—Questions, Anyone?
Say: **Now it's time to see what questions and comments Tommy and the others have about creation.**
Hand out copies of Worksheet 5A "We've Got Questions." Let students skim the worksheet to see what they should look for in the video. Play segment two of *How Now Shall We Live? Student Edition Video*. Stop the VCR before Colson's comments. Ask students to compare notes from their worksheets. The answers to the worksheet questions are:
1. Tommy
2. the Isolation Chamber
3. "admit to the obvious and I don't want to"
4. Darwin puts popcorn into his scientific mixture and says he has produced life from a chemical concoction. Darwin also puts his fingers in his ears and refuses to hear the truth.
5. that he wasn't being honest.

Ask students:
• **What did Tommy mean by his question that sent him to the Isolation Chamber?** (The question is printed on Worksheet 5A.)
• **How do you feel about Darwin's theory and those who continue to support Darwin's beliefs?**
• **Why do scientists (and others) continue to look for an explanation of creation that doesn't include God?**

Direct students to page 34 in the Student Edition. Ask volunteers to share the questions they wrote in the first column. Ask: **What other questions do you have about this week's study?**

Say: **Let's see what Charles Colson brings to our discussion.** Play the Colson interview of segment two on the Student Edition Video.

> ADDITIONALLY . . . 1
> Popcorn plays an important part in this session's video. Hand out small bags of popcorn for the students to munch on as they watch the first video segment.

Enlist a student to read aloud *Genesis 11:1-9*. Tell the others to listen for similarities between the theories they have been discussing and the events of this familiar story in the Bible. After students hear the story of the tower of Babel, ask:
• **What was the people's initial idea for the tower?**
• **What caused the people to lose their focus?**
• **How did God handle the situation?**
• **What similarities do you see between the story and the various theories about creation?** (Tried to get along without God; building something, but leaving God out of it.)

Step 4—Experience Creation
Use these last two steps to focus students on the God of all creation. If the weather permits, plan on doing the last two activities outside. (Take copies of Worksheet 5B "Doxology" and your Bible with you.)

If possible, walk to five different locations during this activity. If not, pick a place where students can see God's world around them.
• Walk to the first location. Tell students to call out different sights they SEE that remind them of God's design in creation.
• Move to a second area. Direct students to remain quiet for several minutes as they HEAR God's creation. Ask students to call out the different noises that remind them of God's purpose.
• Stroll to a third area. In this place direct students to close their eyes and sniff. Ask them to share the odors they SMELL, recognizing that some of these may not be pleasant. Invite students to identify these smells.

Ask: **How can odors, even unpleasant ones, remind you of God's divine creation?**
• At the fourth site, direct students to walk around and TOUCH different objects. Call them together and ask them to share the different textures they felt. Invite volunteers to share how these various textures remind them of a divine creation.
• Finally, at the fifth area have a basket or bowl of fruit or vegetables for students to TASTE. Ask: **How does your sense of taste help you see God's design and purpose for everything on earth?** Read *Romans 1:20* aloud to students.

> OPTION 3
> If you can't go outside, use this alternate activity. Direct students to the last two questions in Day Five, page 52 of the Student Edition. Invite students to share what they wrote for these two questions. Encourage them to share stories about times when God's creation really helped them realize there is a God. Or, ask them to tell about specific wonders in God's world that intrigue them, such as a spider's web.

LEAVING PREPARED (5 minutes)
Step 5—Worship God
You can do this activity outside, as well as inside. Gather students into an informal circle so they can hear each other.

Say: **You've looked at ideas and theories this week that have stretched your mind. As we've seen, some of these theories are even hard for scientists to grasp.**

Reflect back on any particular moment or activity during this session that seemed to be a moment of insight or revelation for students. State that the only true way to honor God and to thank Him for His divine creation is to worship Him. Hand out copies of Worksheet 5B "Doxology." Explain that after students read this doxology aloud together, they should look to the heavens and shout either a name of God *(Yahweh, Elohim, Lord)*, a characteristic of God that relates to creation *(Master Craftsman, Divine Designer, Caring Creator)*, or a brief two or three word prayer. Read the doxology in unison, then shout the closing prayer.

> OPTION 4
> If you stay inside, here's an alternate activity to the shouted prayer. Gather students into an informal circle so they can hear each other.
> Say: **You've looked at ideas and theories this week that have stretched your mind. As we've seen, some of these theories are even hard for scientists to grasp.**
> Reflect back on any particular moment or activity during this session that seemed to be a moment of

insight or revelation for students. State that the only true way to honor God and to thank Him for His divine creation is to worship Him. Hand out copies of Worksheet 5B "Doxology" and pencils. Direct students to turn the sheet over, and write a brief two- or three-sentence prayer. Invite volunteers to share their prayers. Lead students to read the verses of this New Testament doxology in unison. After the reading, tell students to quietly whisper their prayers to God. When all are through, simply say: **Amen.**

UNIT THREE

Science or Religion?

Session Goals
This session is designed to help students:
• examine evidence that evolution is a religious belief system;
• recognize the tendency to believe science over the supernatural;
• determine how naturalistic thought destroys truth, justice, and moral law.

Session Overview
Step 1: Video Summary—Summarize the video clip in one sentence.
Step 2: Look for Evidence—Identify specifics of naturalism and theism (one God) through a relay race.
Step 3: Dig Deeper—Understand the different statements through discussion and Bible study.
Step 4: Colson's Interview—View Charles Colson's explanation of both worldviews and compare to students' ideas.
Step 5: Challenge Students' Beliefs—Challenge words and concepts others may not understand in students' beliefs.
Step 6: Why?—Work on memory verse to express why it's important to understand others' worldviews.

Before the Session
GATHER:
❏ extra Bibles

for Step 1
❏ *How Now Shall We Live? Student Edition Video*
❏ TV-VCR
❏ paper, pencils

for Step 2
❏ Worksheet 6 "Statements of Worldviews"
❏ construction paper, marker, masking tape

for Step 5
❏ *How Now Shall We Live? Student Edition Video*
❏ TV-VCR
❏ large sheet of paper, marker

DO:
for Step 2
❏ Duplicate Worksheet 6 "Statements of Worldviews." You will need one copy of the statements for each relay team. (HINT: Duplicate each team's statements on a different color of paper.)
❏ Cut the statements apart.
❏ Make a set of three signs for each relay team. The signs are: *Christianity, Naturalism, Neutral.* Tape these to the wall in front of each relay team.

for Additionally . . . 1
❏ Make a set of signs and statements from the worksheet for each student

During the Session

GETTING INVOLVED (10 minutes)
Step 1—Video Summary
Begin the session by showing the third segment of *How Now Shall We Live? Student Edition Video*. Before starting the video, tell students to watch the video carefully, because they will be asked to summarize its content at the end of the video. Play the video segment, stopping the tape before the interview with Colson.

Hand out paper and pencils. Direct each student to write a one-sentence summary of what they watched. Call for students to share their statements.

Say: **Perhaps you feel as confused as Tommy. This has been a tough week of study. You've looked at statements with difficult words. You've studied complex ideas that are hard to grasp. But, you've made it through the week. Congratulations! Today let's check out several of those difficult ideas.**

FOCUSING ON THE FACTS (35 minutes)
Step 2—Look for Evidence
Say: **Your challenge this week was to look for evidence that evolution is not as much about science as it is about religion.** Ask:
• **Why should a Christian know the basics of evolutionary theory and the evidence against it?**
• **How can you tell the difference between a scientific fact and a religious belief?**
• **What "evidence" did you find during your study that evolution is being presented as a religion, instead of as a scientific study?**

Encourage students to refer to the Student Edition to find statements and ideas to support their answers to these questions.

Before the session, duplicate Worksheet 6 "Statements of Worldviews." Also, prepare three construction paper signs for each team. The signs are: *Naturalism, Christianity, Neutral.* Tape these signs to a wall opposite where the teams will line up.

Divide students into two or more equal teams for a relay race. Line up each relay team across from a set of three signs. Explain that you will hand the first person on each team a sentence from this week's study. The student races to the opposite wall and decides whether the statement expresses a *naturalist* point of view, a *Christian* point of view, or is a *neutral* sentence of general interest. Inform students that there are only two *neutral* statements. After taping the first sentence under a heading, the first student races back to tag a second student who receives another sentence to classify as either *Naturalism, Christianity,* or *Neutral.* After all statements have been taped under one of the three signs, briefly compare the different placements from team to team. Although the answers are given below, do not correct which statements go under which signs at this time. That will take place in Steps 3 and 4.

ADDITIONALLY . . 1
If you have less than four students (2 students could make a relay team), give each student a stack of statements from Worksheet 6 and the three categories *(Naturalism, Christianity, Neutral).* Tell each student to race against the clock to see who can put each statement under the correct heading.

Here are the answers and page numbers in the Student Edition where you can find these statements. Several statements have been reworded. A couple of statements came from the Student Edition Video which they watched in Step 1.

1. Naturalistic, page 55
2. Neutral, page 57
3. Christian, (*Psalm 111:10*), also page 58
4. Neutral, page 60
5. Christian, page 64
6. Naturalistic, page 66
7. Naturalistic, page 69
8. Christian, page 65
9. Christian, page 65
10. Naturalistic, video
11. Christian, page 70
12. Naturalistic, page 66
13. Naturalistic, video
14. Naturalistic, page 68
15. Christian, *Revelation 1:8*

Step 3—Dig Deeper
Discuss the belief statements further. Point out statements 1 and 15. Ask:
• **Why does statement 1 sound like a religious statement?** (Can't be proven, has a similar structure as a liturgy or biblical statement such as *Rev. 1:8*.)

Remind students that this particular statement was regularly used by Carl Sagan in his TV programs and in his writings.

Invite students to choose other statements that may have caused confusion or that contradict each other. For example, ask:
• **Why does statement 5 go under the Christianity heading?** (If that's where students placed it).

Invite students to question the placement of other statements. Assign students to look up those questionable statements in the Student Edition (give them the page numbers) to find supporting comments for the placement of each statement.

Focus specifically on statement 8. Direct students to turn to *Galatians 5:19-23* in their Bibles and to page 65 in the Student Edition. Ask students to name the behaviors they marked as natural outgrowths of a naturalistic worldview. Challenge students to identify a specific way each negative behavior may develop from naturalist thought. For example, ask:
• **How would sexual immorality develop based on the ideas and statements you have heard and studied about naturalism?**
• **How do the positive attitudes and actions in verses 22-23 develop from Christianity?**
• **How does Christianity set you free?**
• **Why is accountability to God important to a person?**
• **How does naturalism eliminate divine law or ultimate authority?**

ADDITIONALLY . . . 2
If you have more than an hour for this session, direct students to *Matthew 4:1-11.* Say: **On Day Five you looked at this Scripture, identifying the opponents and what was at stake.**
  Direct students to turn to page 67 in the Student Edition and to share their thoughts on how Satan's temptations would appeal to the pragmatist and to one who believes in relativity. Ask:
• **How does an economic savior fit the idea of naturalism?**
• **How does a savior with personal, selfish ambitions go along with the beliefs of naturalism?**
• **How does a savior with great power support naturalism?**
• **How did Christ's responses show us a biblical worldview?**

• **What would you say to a friend who says, "I can believe in both evolution (naturalism) and Christianity at the same time. One's a scientific explanation and the other's a biblical explanation of creation"?**

Step 4—Colson's Interview

Play the interview with Charles Colson from the third segment of the Student Edition Video. Colson shares his ideas about naturalism and theism (belief in God) in everyday language, giving characteristics and examples. Challenge your students to listen carefully to what Colson says. After the video, invite students to change any sentence strips from Step 2, until each statement is under its related sign.

> ADDITIONALLY . . . 3
>
> If you have more than an hour for this session, direct students to "Cosmos or Creation?" on page 68 of the Student Edition. Tell half the students to notice the arguments of Yellow, while the other half studies the arguments of Pink. Direct students to build a case for their puppet's point of view. Students can use ideas expressed in the last three weeks of study. Call for each team's arguments.

Step 5—Challenge Students' Beliefs

Using the back of the paper from Step 1, direct students to write down two or three statements or phrases about their personal beliefs. Offer ideas such as: a statement about your conversion, what you believe about God, what you believe about prayer, how you feel about forgiveness. After a few minutes, invite volunteers to share their statements aloud. As they share, write on a large sheet of paper religious words your students use that might not be understood by someone who has never been in church. For example, list words and phrases like *conversion, sin, forgiveness, grace, personal Savior, Lord of my life.* After several students have shared, point to different words on the list. Challenge students to explain the term or phrase in non-religious language. Ask:

• **What is pre-evangelism?** (A definition is given on page 70 in the Student Edition.)

Direct a student to read the paragraph after the first two questions on page 70 of the Student Edition. (The opening sentence begins "The best way of fighting the religion of naturalism . . .") Ask:

• **What does this mean?**
• **How can someone defeat another's belief "on its own turf"?**

Direct all students to turn to *Acts 17:16-34* in their Bibles. Invite three students to read this passage—one as the narrator, one representing the voices of the people, and one as Paul. After the reading tell students to turn to pages 70-71 in the Student Edition. As you read each of the questions beginning at the bottom of page 70 ("According to *verses 32-34*, what three reactions . . ."), call on different students to share what they wrote for each study question.

Encourage students to share personal stories of friends who don't know what sin is, or who never have heard about Jesus except as a cuss word. Perhaps one of your students came from a non-Christian environment and would be willing to share.

> OPTION 1
>
> If you work with older students, use this option to replace Step 5. Direct students to the four statements on page 68 of the Student Edition ("When mammals die, they are really and truly dead . . ."). After reading each statement, call on students to find Scripture that gives the Christian point of view. For example for the first statement "When mammals die. . ." look at *1 Corinthians 15* for verses to refute this statement. Also, direct students to answer the two questions below the four statements ("Why is Darwinism such a dangerous idea? What 'non-scientific' areas of life does it threaten to destroy?").

LEAVING PREPARED (5 minutes)
Step 6—Why?

Say: **Maybe you have struggled in understanding this material. Perhaps you have friends and family who seem to get along by believing in both evolution and a God-created universe. Or, you may not care, because you don't see how you can use this information. Let's make a quick internal investigation.**

Direct a student to read *Matthew 5:13-14*. Invite students to recall what they said about being salt and light to the world. Ask:

• **How does this verse answer the question of why we need to learn about evolution and these other theories?**

Repeat the *Matthew 5:13-14* in unison. Then, tell students to turn to a partner and repeat the verses by memory. Explain that these first three weeks of study have answered the first worldview question: Where did we come from and who are we? Close the session by inviting students to pray.

UNIT FOUR
The Fall

Session Goals
This session is designed to help students:
• look at the second worldview question—What has gone wrong with the world?
• study the Christian view of sin and evil;
• compare the Christian view to other belief systems.

Session Overview
Step 1: Gotta Believe Check-Up—Determine which statements express a personal belief system on evil.
Step 2: A "Sad" Report—Hear a "sad lib" on the first sin.
Step 3: The Campaign Trail—Examine the differences between Christianity and other belief systems' view of sin.
Step 4: "It's Not My Fault!"—Discover how to handle the excuses of sin.
Step 5: Gotta Believe Re-Check—Review personal beliefs about sin.

Before the Session
GATHER:
❏ extra Bibles

for visual support
❏ the three-question visual from Unit One

for Step 1
❏ Worksheet 7 "Gotta Believe Check-up"
❏ pencils
❏ upbeat contemporary Christian music CD
❏ CD player

for Additionally . . . 1
❏ construction paper, marker

for Option 1
❏ construction paper, marker
❏ newspapers, news magazines

for Step 3
❏ Worksheet 8 "The Campaign Trail"
❏ pencils
❏ art supplies like construction paper, scissors, glue or tape, yarn, markers

for Option 3
❏ paper, pencils

for Step 4
❏ *How Now Shall We Live? Student Edition Video*

❏ TV-VCR
❏ large sheet of paper, markers

DO:
for Step 1
❏ Duplicate Worksheet 7 "Gotta Believe Check-Up."

for Additionally . . . 1
❏ Make signs (*I Believe, I Don't Believe*).

for Option 1
❏ Make the suggested sign *No God. No sin. No guilt. No problem!*

for Step 3
❏ Duplicate Worksheet 8 "The Campaign Trail."

During the Session

GETTING INVOLVED (15 minutes)
Step 1—Gotta Believe Check-Up
As students arrive, hand each a copy of Worksheet 7 "Gotta Believe Check-Up" and a pencil. Direct students to follow the instructions on the sheet. Play upbeat music as students work on their papers. Say: **This week you looked at several belief systems as you began to answer the second worldview question—"What has gone wrong with the world?" During this session we will clarify what you studied. Hold on to your "Gotta Believe Check-Up" worksheet until the end of the session.** Display the three-question visual from Unit One.

ADDITIONALLY . . . 1
If you have active students, they may prefer to move around. Hand out copies of Worksheet 7 "Gotta Believe Check-Up" and pencils. Choose five statements from the worksheet to use in this activity. Designate one side of the room as "I believe." Designate the opposite side of the room as "I don't believe." (You might want to make signs for both sides of the room.) Read a statement from the worksheet, then direct students to walk to the side of the room that best expresses his or her belief. Some students may want to stand along a continuum between the two designated walls. After each statement, challenge students to defend their choices. Having the statements printed on a worksheet will help students make their choices quickly without having to ask for the sentence to be read repeatedly.

Step 2—A "Sad" Report
Explain that you need the help of your students. You are working on a story, but you are missing a few words. Ask for the words as described in brackets. Write in the word suggested by your students. Do not read the information

outside the brackets at this time.

Now the [type of animal] was more [an adjective] than any of the wild animals the LORD God had made. He said to the woman, "Did [name of someone important] really say, 'You must not [active verb] from any [noun associated with the out-of-doors] in the garden'?"

The woman said to the serpent, "We may eat [something found in a grocery store] from the trees in the [a place], but God did say, 'You must not eat fruit from the tree that is in the [a position] of the [another place], and you must not [one of the five senses] it, or you will [active verb].' "

"You will not surely [another active verb]," the serpent said to the woman. "For God knows that when you eat of it your [a part of your face] will be opened, and you will be like God, knowing [two opposite adjectives]."

When the woman saw that the [something else from a grocery store] of the [something in a forest] was [adjective] for food and pleasing to the eye, and also desirable for gaining [something every student wants], she took some and [active verb] it. She also gave some to her [family member], who was with her, and he [active verb] it. (Based on *Gen. 3:1-6*)

After getting all the words, tell students you want to read them the completed story. Read the verses from *Genesis 3:1-6* with the "sad lib" words. Direct students to turn to *Genesis 3:1-6* in their Bibles and read the "real" version. Say: **Maybe this week you had times when you felt like you were reading a "sad lib" because the words and thoughts were difficult to understand. Hopefully, we can help you sort through these ideas.**
Ask:
• **Why is Genesis 3 called "The Fall"?**
• **Why did God place an untouchable tree in His perfect creation to tempt Adam and Eve? Was it temptation?**
• **How has this sin by Adam and Eve corrupted all humans?**
• **Is it easier or harder to accept sin as the source of the problems in this world? Defend your point of view.**
Say: **Even Adam and Eve had trouble accepting that they had sinned. Invite a student to read Genesis 3:12-13.**
Ask:
• **Who did the man blame for his sin?**
• **Who did the woman blame for her sin?**
• **How do you see this blame game acted out in society today?**
• **What questions do you have about sin?**
• **Does believing in God help you face sin or ignore it?**

OPTION 1
Replace the "sad lib" writing activity with this idea. Prior to the session make a sign that says *No God. No sin. No guilt. No problem!* Display the sign at this time. Hand out copies of newspapers and news magazines. Direct students to find examples to refute or support these statements in news stories, advertisements, TV programs, Dear Ann/Abby letters. For example, students might look for news stories of people blaming others, without taking personal responsibility for their own actions. Call on students to share their newspaper/news magazine examples. Continue with the study of *Genesis 3*.

FOCUSING ON THE FACTS (25 minutes)
Step 3—The Campaign Trail
State that students are going on the campaign trail. (Even though this may not be an election year in your area, someone somewhere is being elected to something!) Divide students into two teams and call them campaign committees. Both campaign committees are trying to get their leader elected. Both candidates are running on a platform that completes the statement: The Problem with the World Today is . . .

Hand out copies of Worksheet 8 "The Campaign Trail" and pencils. Tell one campaign committee to build a campaign around a Christian candidate, facing the reality of sin as the corrupting ingredient that causes today's problems (such as murders, thieves, violence, alcohol, teen pregnancies, etc.). Tell the other campaign committee to build a campaign around a Utopian candidate, who believes the utopian ideas you studied this week. Suggest committees create a slogan for their candidate that tells each candidate's point of view. Campaign committees can also design banners, make up a campaign song, write a 30-second TV commercial, and outline a brief platform speech on what their candidate believes. Provide art supplies for these activities. Tell campaign committees to use Scripture to "back up" their campaign points. Tell the Utopian campaign committee to use the Scripture, but to distort the verses for its own purposes. Encourage students to look back at this past week's studies to find ideas and themes.

Call for each campaign committee's presentation. Ask students to decide which candidate their friends would support.

OPTION 2
Replace this step with a debate. There are several excellent statements from the week's study. Here are a few:
• Ignoring human sin makes life and society not better but uncontrollably worse. (p. 75 in the Student Edition)

- Human nature is good until it is corrupted by society. (p. 78 in the Student Edition)
- Because things cannot be described scientifically, therefore, they are not real. (p. 84 in the Student Edition)

Select a topic. Divide into two teams and let each side defend its point of view.

OPTION 3

For students who enjoy creative writing, use this activity, instead of Step 3. Say: **You have seen in your studies this week that belief systems other than Christianity try to explain what's wrong with the world by distorting truth.**

Hand out paper and pencils. Challenge students to rewrite the following Scriptures from a Utopian point of view. This would be a paraphrase of the Scripture from a reverse point of view. The references are:

Proverbs 19:1
John 8:32
Romans 6:23
Proverbs 19:18
Romans 1:21-22

Call for students to share their "new" Scripture verses. Direct students to look at the Scripture as the "new" verses are read so they can see the distortions. If you have time, let them compare the before and after Scriptures. Invite students to share new insights they gained from writing these verses in a reverse paraphrase.

MAKING IT REAL (15 minutes)
Step 4—"It's Not My Fault!"
Play the fourth segment of the Student Edition Video, including the interview with Charles Colson. Direct students to listen for the excuses different people use in deciding what's wrong with this world. Suggest they make notes on the back of their worksheets. When the video ends, call on students to identify the excuses they heard in the video. List these on a large sheet of paper. Now, ask students to identify other "excuses" they make or that they hear others make. (Students might include these: "It's not my job"; "I thought it was OK"; "I didn't know"; "I can't control what happened"; "I'm the victim here"; "He made me do it.") Urge students to suggest ways to face up to these excuses.

ADDITIONALLY . . . 2
If you have more than an hour for this session, use these case studies to help your students see how to talk with friends and family about what they are learning. Read each case study, letting different students suggest solutions.

Case Study 1—I'm getting really tired of being teased by older students. I have just as much right to walk down the hall as they do. Why won't they leave me alone? Next time someone pushes me around they'll be asking for it; and they're gonna get it!

Case Study 2—It's not fair. We were a happy family until mom decided to leave. She said she couldn't take it any more, but never said what "it" was. Now I have to do the cleaning and cooking and watching after my little brother when I should be free to play on the school team or hang out with my friends.

Case Study 3—How did I know the police would bust up that party. It was a private party; we weren't hurting anyone. Why do the cops get so bent out of shape when we're just blowing off a week of school? I bet the police let loose on their time off. Anyway, I told my parents I didn't know alcohol was going to be served or I wouldn't have gone. They always believe me.

LEAVING PREPARED (5 minutes)
Step 5—Gotta Believe Re-Check
Direct students to look again at Worksheet 7 "Gotta Believe Check-Up." Direct students to check in the second column which statements they believe are true. Ask:
- **Which statements did you change your answer to and why?**
- **Which statements on the worksheet are really excuses offered by other belief systems or philosophies?**
- **What one thing can you say or do this week to take responsibility for personal sin?**

Pray for the students. Thank God for His redemption and love.

Redemption and The Myth of Progress

Session Goals
This session is designed to help students:
- understand the desire for spiritual redemption;
- explore several forms of redemption offered in today's culture;
- determine if these redemptive ideas fit into a Christian worldview.

Session Overview
Step 1: From Darkness to Light—Examine the story of Nicky Cruz, especially his movement from darkness to light.

Step 2: Redemption Formulas—Match philosophers with theories and evaluate how each would answer the worldview questions.

Step 3: On Second Thought!—Note worldview comments from *How Now Shall We Live? Student Edition Video*

Step 4: Going Up?—Graph a personal "escalator" of life.

Step 5: The Results of Sexual Liberation—Discuss who gets hurt in the sexual liberation.

Before the Session
GATHER:
❑ extra Bibles

for visual support
❑ the three-question visual from Unit One in *How Now Shall We Live? Student Edition*

for Step 1
❑ large sheets of paper, markers

for Additionally . . . 1
❑ video of Nicky Cruz
The Cross and the Switchblade or *Run Baby Run* (Both videos can be ordered from *www.nicky cruz.org/* the Nicky Cruz Outreach Organization on the web, or 719-598-2600 in Colorado. Your church media center or a Christian bookstore near you also may have the videos.)
❑ TV-VCR

for Step 2
❑ Worksheet *9* "Cards and Questions"

for Option 1
❑ construction paper, glue, scissors, markers
❑ general pictures from magazines

for Option 2
❑ paper, pens
❑ index cards

for Step 3
❑ How *Now Shall We Live? Student Edition Video*
❑ TV-VCR
❑ Worksheet 10 "Duh?!"

for Step 4
❑ large sheets of paper, markers
❑ paper, pencils

for Step 5
❑ construction paper, glue, scissors, markers

for Additionally . . . 3
❑ *Speechless* CD (Steven Curtis Chapman, Sparrow Records, Inc.)
❑ CD player

DO:
for Step 1
❑ Set up the room as suggested.

for Step 2
❑ Duplicate Worksheet *9* "Cards and Questions." Cut apart the cards on *9*. Make enough copies of the bottom of *9* for every student to have a copy.

for Additionally . . . 2
❑ Call or e-mail students to bring in the suggested school books.

For Step 3
❑ Duplicate Worksheet 10 "Duh?!"

During the Session

GETTING INVOLVED (10 minutes)
Step 1—From Darkness to Light
Set up the chairs in two separate groups. If possible, turn off the lights in part of the room where one group will sit. As students arrive, direct half to one group and half to the other. Tell one group they represent darkness; the other group represents light. Ask someone from the "Darkness Group" to read *Isaiah 5:20* aloud. Direct someone from the "Light Group" to read *Matthew 5:13-14*. Give each group a large sheet of paper and a marker.

Tell each group to review "The Story of Nicky Cruz" on page 91 of *How Now Shall We Live? Student Edition*. Instruct the "Darkness Group" to list ways Cruz lived in darkness. Tell the "Light Group" to list ways Cruz walks in the light.

After groups have reported, say: **This week you began to answer the third question of our three worldview questions.**

Point out the three-questions visual used in Units One and Four. Ask:

• **How does the story of Nicky Cruz answer the second and third worldview questions? (What has gone wrong with the world? What can we do to fix it?)**
• **Which worldview does Cruz live with his life right now? Support your answer with examples.**
• **How does the story of Nicky Cruz show that there is a way to fix what's wrong with the world?**

Explain that the light of Jesus Christ helps us be salt and light in the world as His representatives. Lead students to repeat *Matthew 5:13-14* from memory. Begin with a prayer for light and understanding during this session.

> ADDITIONALLY . . . 1
> If you have more than an hour for this session, show a part of Nicky Cruz's life story as portrayed in the video *The Cross and the Switchblade* or the documentary *Run Baby Run*. Select a portion of the video to show during the session. Plan a fellowship to watch the remainder of the video. Use the questions above to discuss the video.

FOCUSING ON THE FACTS (30 minutes)
Step 2—Redemption Formulas
Hand out the cards from Worksheet *9* "Characters and Questions." These contain the names and theories of the people students studied this week. If you have more than 14 students, duplicate the top half of the worksheet several times. Each person needs one card. (If you have less that 14 students, give out the name cards, and let students find the related theory cards from those placed on a table.) Direct students to find the person or theory that matches the card they are holding. Once students are paired off, hand each a copy of the "Questions" part of Worksheet *9*.

Applaud students' commitment to stick with this study of philosophies and theories. Explain that today students will apply their week-long study to the three worldview questions. Point out the three-question visual from Units One and Four. Encourage students to use their Student Edition books to complete the "Questions" worksheet based on the theories of their person. Students who have Rousseau and Freud can look back at previous weeks to find additional information. (Here

are page numbers where information begins in the Student Edition for each person: Hegel, p. 92; Marx, p. 95; Rosseau, p. 78; Freud, p. 83; Sanger, p. 101; Kinsey, p. 102; Reich, p. 104.) After a few minutes of study, let each pair present its person and answer the worldview questions. Encourage other students to add their understanding about the person. Ask:

• **Why is it important to know these different philosophies?**
• **How do the answers of these men and women compare to a Christian's answers to these three worldview questions?**
• **How do you see these beliefs affecting today's students? (For example, How are the ideas on sexuality influencing young people?)**
• **What Scripture directly refutes each person's theory?**

If students can't think of Scripture, assign students to read the following verses: *Genesis 11:4; Leviticus 16:10; Proverbs 6:32; Isaiah 53:4-6; Matthew 19:4-5; Matthew 24:4-5; John 3:19-20; Romans 1:18; 1 Corinthians 6:12-20;* and *1 Corinthians 13:4-7.*

> ADDITIONALLY . . . 2
> If you have more than an hour for this session, try this activity. Before the session, call or e-mail several students, asking them to bring in their school books—either their science books, sociology books, or books that have sex education information. During the session direct students to look up the different people in their school books to see how their beliefs and philosophies are presented. Compare what they find from their textbooks with their work in the Student Edition this week.

> OPTION 1
> Creative students might prefer to do an art activity. Using the information they gathered from this week's study, challenge each pair of students to design a "website" for its assigned person. Provide construction paper, markers, glue, and general pictures from magazines. Students could design a home page with several links.

> OPTION 2
> After answering the worldview questions for their assigned person, direct each pair of students to create a business card or personal logo for the person. Hand out index cards to use as business cards. Provide paper and markers for development of the logo. Call on volunteers to share. Continue with the main questions in this step.

Step 3—On Second Thought!
Say: **Now it's time to see what Tommy's been up to. Listen to the statements Tommy makes to refute the words of Darwin, Marx, and others.**

Play the *How Now Shall We Live? Student Edition Video* through Charles Colson's interview. Hand out copies of Worksheet 10 "Duh?!" Explain that these are quotes from the video. Ask students to explain how they might respond to the comments of Bark and Karl Marx. Ask students to choose a quote from Tommy or Bark or Marx and decide how they might share this information with a Christian friend. Challenge students to think of ways to share these thoughts with non-Christian friends.

MAKING IT REAL (10 minutes)
Step 4—Going Up?
Say: **You started out the week looking at one myth of progress identified by one philosopher as "the Escalator Fallacy." Who can explain Hegel's theory about life?**

Direct students to page 94 in the Student Edition if they need to refresh their memories. Invite students to draw on a large sheet of paper their understanding of what this progressive myth looks like. One example is on page 94, but students might have other ideas. Ask:
• **Why is this called a fallacy?**
• **Where does Christianity fit into this view of progress?**

Hand out paper and pencils. Challenge students to draw the events in their lives using a ladder, an escalator, or any other object that will explain their lives. Remind students to include things they've done that lifted them upward toward God, and acts that made them face reality. Encourage them to identify a time when Jesus Christ became real to them and how God has helped them move through life. Invite a student to read *John 14:6*. Ask:
• **How does this verse compare to Hegel's idea that we are moving toward a "glorious completion"?**
• **What is the glorious completion for a Christian?**

> OPTION 3
> If you chose Option 1 where students created websites for the philosophers they studied, allow them to design a personal website at this time. Suggest students include statements, Scripture, pictures, and links that would let a visitor to that website know that this person was a Christian. Let volunteers share their personal website designs.

> ADDITIONALLY . . . 3
> If you have more than an hour for this session, play "The Change" (Steven Curtis Chapman, *Speechless*, Sparrow Records, Inc.). Challenge students to listen for all the trappings that make the outside of a person look like a Christian. Invite students to identify what brings the change, and what that change involves. Discuss how the song relates to the theories and philosophies you've been studying.

LEAVING PREPARED (10 minutes)
Step 5—The Results of Sexual Liberation
Ask:
• **Of the ideas examined today, which ones are impacting your life and the lives of your friends?**
• **How do some of these theories impact today's culture?**
• **How is the idea of "sex is salvation" being lived out by many students across America?**
• **What is the Christian's response to the sexual revolution?**
• **What are some of the results of sexual liberation?**

Share this information from Colson's book *How Now Shall We Live?*
• The National Survey of Family Growth found that women who were not virgins when they got married have a 71 percent higher divorce rate.[1]

• About 90 percent of the couples who live together say they want to get married, but the National Survey of Families and Households found that almost half break up before signing a marriage license. Those who do marry are 50 percent more likely to divorce.[2]

• Crime and substance abuse are strongly linked to fatherless households. Studies show that 60 percent of rapists grew up in fatherless homes, as did 72 percent of adolescent murderers and 70 percent of all long-term prison inmates.[3]

• One in four have a sexually transmitted disease.[4] Human papilloma virus (HPV), a STD for which there is no cure, infects 5.5 million new cases a year, many of them young adults.[5]

Conclude the study by reminding students that God offers forgiveness, redemption, and hope. Students will study these important messages in the coming weeks. Read *Psalm 17:6-8* and *Hebrews 4:14-16* as a closing prayer.

[1] Charles Colson, *How Now Shall We Live?* (Wheaton, IL: Tyndale House Publishers, 1999), 327.

[2] Ibid, 327.

[3] Ibid, 323.

[4] Ibid, 243.

[5] "Better Safe Than Sorry," *Newsweek Special Issue,* Spring/ Summer 1999, 54.

UNIT SIX
Real Redemption

Session Goals
This session is designed to help students:
- continue to compare Christianity to other belief systems;
- identify the easy, but inadequate, solutions that other religions use in dealing with sin and guilt;
- gain an accurate picture of the only answer for sin.

Session Overview
Step 1: A Buffet of Beliefs—Note the variety of messages from different worldviews.

Step 2: Think About This—Discuss different statements from their study.

Step 3: God is WHAT?—Consider how different belief systems would answer basic religious questions.

Step 4: Tough Choices—Check out the choices faced in deciding what to believe.

Step 5: It's In the Bag—Consider what is needed to help others understand Christianity.

Before the Session
GATHER:
❑ extra Bibles

for Step 1
❑ *War of the Worlds* video
❑ *How Now Shall We Live? Student Edition Video*
❑ TV-VCR
❑ index cards
❑ pencils
❑ large sheets of paper
❑ markers

for Option 2
❑ large sheets of paper
❑ markers

for Step 3
❑ Worksheet 11 "God is . . ."

for Step 4
❑ Worksheet 12 "Would You Rather?"

for Step 5
❑ small paper bags
❑ white paper

for Option 4
❑ sculpting items like pipe cleaners, paper clips, lightweight wire, construction paper

DO:
for Step 1
❑ Rent the video *War of the Worlds*.

for Option 1
❑ Write statements from Unit Six on slips of paper.

for Step 3
❑ Duplicate Worksheet 11 "God is . . ."

for Step 4
❑ Duplicate Worksheet 12 "Would You Rather?" and cut the cards apart

During the Session

GETTING INVOLVED (10 minutes)
Step 1—A Buffet of Beliefs
Rent *War of the Worlds* from a local video store. Preview the film prior to the session. As students arrive, show the portion of the video mentioned in the Day One study on page 111 of *How Now Shall We Live? Student Edition.* Point out the video and encourage students to watch and comment as they choose. Invite comparison to *Independence Day* which many of your students probably saw.

Start the session by stating that this week students examined a buffet of beliefs. Explain that now they will see those summarized. Hand out index cards and pencils. Before starting this video, tell students to identify and make notes about the different belief systems presented in the video. Show the *How Now Shall We Live? Student Edition Video* up to the Colson interview. After the video, call for each belief system and a brief definition. The ones mentioned in the video are: science (provable, genetic changes), outer space (extraterrestrials), eastern mystic (New Age), intellectualism ("institutionalized naturalism"), hedonism (self-indulgence), goth (life is dark and pointless), Christianity. After playing the video, let students call out the different belief system as you list them on a large sheet of paper. Ask:
- **How did you feel about the way Christianity was presented?**
- **Why do you think it was presented in that way?**
- **Why do these belief systems appeal to people today?**

- **Why do people look to science?**
- **Why have people been so excited about the findings in genetics?**
- **How do you feel about extraterrestrials? If there are space aliens do you think they are more advanced or less advanced than we are? Why?**

As students comment, write brief phrases about each belief system's appeal on the list.

FOCUSING ON THE FACTS (30 minutes)
Step 2—Think About This
After making the list, suggest students flip back through this week's study looking for statements or ideas that made them think. Let volunteers read these statements or ideas aloud. Invite others to share their points of view about the chosen statements. Here are several statements that students might discuss. Page numbers reference where the statement is located in the Student Edition.

"...the highest stage is the scientific stage, where people find truth through scientific experimentation." (p. 113)

"Why can science not provide a standard of values?" (p. 115)

"If we can do it, we should." (p. 116)

(SETI) is "'A dream based on faith—a technological search for God.'" (p. 117)

"Humanity's problems are not related to wrong moral choices but to lack of knowledge." (p. 117)

"'The more the universe seems comprehensible (understandable), the more it also seems pointless.'" (p. 118)

(Jean-Paul Sarte said of God,) "'Failing to take root in my heart, He vegetated in me for a while, then He died.'" (p. 119)

(E. O. Wilson's) "goal is to make religion subject to science or naturalism." (p. 122)

"Various meditation exercises are sold as means for resolving conflict and for enhancing relaxation, creativity, self-esteem, and even physical health." (p. 125)

Students may have several comments to make about the New Age material presented in Day Four, since this religious movement has permeated so much of today's society. After students have shared their statements, direct

one student to read *Matthew 6:19-21* in a Bible. Ask:
- **What treasures do other belief systems seek?**
- **What treasures do these belief systems find?**
- **How does a Christian belief system reflect that person's treasures?**
- **How does it help you better understand your faith to study other religious beliefs?**

OPTION 1
If students prefer something more active, let them do impromptu scenes related to the different statements. On separate slips of paper write several statements of your choosing from this week's study, or use those statements suggested above. Fold up these slips of paper. Let students pick a statement and either act out the idea alone or involve one or two others in an impromptu skit. The other students should try to guess the general idea behind the statement.

OPTION 2
If students enjoy musical activities, use this idea. Assign each belief system (or each day's study) to a team of students. Tell them to write new words to a familiar chorus, hymn, or jingle for their assigned religion. Give each team a large sheet of paper and a marker to use in recording their new words. Let each team lead the others in singing the new song. For example, the team looking at Day Two's study might choose the chorus "Awesome God", writing new words like "Our god is genetic matter."

Step 3—God is WHAT?
Divide students into five teams—one for each day's study. (Consider including the study of goth and hedonism for older students.) Hand out Worksheet 11 "God is . . ." and pencils. Tell each team to complete the statements based on the belief system they have been assigned. (If you have less than six students, work on the chart as a group.) Call on students to share their assigned belief systems' responses. As each team reports, suggest everyone fill in their worksheets with the information.

ADDITIONALLY . . . 1
If you have more than an hour for this session, work on the last statement on the chart. Students may complete this sentence ("The way to relate to others is . . .") in different ways. Lead them to think about completing the sentence with variations on the Golden Rule *("Do to others as you would have them do to you." Luke 6:31)*. For example, genetics might say, "Do to others to get what is the best for you."

ADDITIONALLY . . . 2

If you have more than an hour for this session, invite students to share several ideas presented in Day Five. Direct them to identify the evidence of Jesus' crucifixion and resurrection introduced in the material on pages 129-130 in the Student Edition. Urge them to use other information they've learned in their own studies of the crucifixion and resurrection. As you do Step 4, comment on the "Would You Rather?" card that asks if students would rather die for a lie or the truth. Ask how that relates to the resurrection. Point out Colson's statements about the Watergate cover-up on pages 129-130. Remind students that Colson eventually was convicted of obstruction of justice in the Watergate scandal that resulted in the resignation of President Richard Nixon.

MAKING IT REAL (10 minutes)

Step 4—Tough Choices

Duplicate and cut apart Worksheet 12 "Would You Rather?" (If you need more than twelve cards, duplicate the worksheet several times, or create your own "Would You Rather?" cards.) Let each student choose a card, answering the question on the card.

Say: **You may not like the choices, but that's the dilemma. Sometimes you have to make a choice when the choices are neither easy nor acceptable.**

Challenge students to defend the choices they make. Invite students to suggest alternate choices, instead of those mentioned on the card.

After everyone has shared a card, direct students to look at the worldview statements they wrote in the front of their Student Editions in the first unit. Direct students to the idea from Daniel Quinn, expressed on page 111 ("The myth goes something like this: . . .). Ask:

• **How would you change your worldview statement based on what you've studied in the past six weeks? Why?**

Direct students to share what they wrote in answer to the question on page 112 in the Student Edition. Play the Colson interview in segment six on the Student Edition Video. Ask:

• **How do Colson's comments relate to your evaluation of your worldview statement?**

ADDITIONALLY . . . 3

If you have more than an hour for this session, share this idea with students. Invite a student to read *Acts 1:7.* Say: **Jesus didn't ask us to be prophets of the future. Instead He wanted us to be witnesses to the past.**
Ask:
• **To what do we bear witness?**
• **How important is a personal witness?**
• **Why is it better to be a witness than a prophet?**

LEAVING PREPARED (10 minutes)

Step 5—It's In the Bag

Say: **You are packing your bags for a worldview trip. This trip will take you into an area where you will meet people who have no idea what Christianity is.**

Hand out small paper sacks and sheets of paper. Tell students to tear the paper in smaller pieces. Direct them to use each piece to write down or draw information to help these people understand Christianity. Remind students to be careful not to use "churchy" terminology that won't communicate to these people. Explain that they can use the Bible for support, but not proof. After a few minutes, let each person share several of the items packed in their bags. State that students must equip themselves to go out into this world where so many religions clamor for others' attention. Ask:

• **How often do you have an opportunity to share your beliefs with others?**
• **When or under what conditions do you share your beliefs with others.**
• **If you don't share your faith with others, why is it difficult?**
• **How difficult is it for you to talk about your faith without using religious terms?**
• **What do you need to do to be more "people-friendly" in sharing your faith?**

Invite students to get with a friend. Ask them to pray for one another as they continue to learn about their own beliefs and those of others.

The Church and Culture

Session Goals

This session is designed to help students:
• examine the influence of friends and culture on Christians;
• take the biblical principles into the marketplace;
• celebrate their faith.

Session Overview

Step 1: Ted or Bill?–Evaluate how answers to worldview questions may change.
Step 2: Influenced?–Determine personal influences.
Step 3: Spiritually Strong–Evaluate how Christians have endured.
Step 4: Do I Fit In?–Look at the cultural mandate personally.
Step 5: Celebrate Jesus!–Celebrate that Jesus is worthy of worship.

Before the Session

GATHER:
❑ extra Bibles

for visual support
❑ visual of worldview questions from Unit One

for Step 1
❑ *How Now Shall We Live? Student Edition Video*
❑ TV-VCR

for Step 2
❑ white paper
❑ pencils
❑ Worksheet 13 "Influenced?"

for Option #1
❑ construction paper
❑ markers

for Step 4
❑ *How Now Shall We Live? Student Edition Video*
❑ TV-VCR
❑ several large sheets of paper
❑ art supplies like construction paper, scissors, markers, masking tape, yarn
❑ Worksheet 14 "A Question of Questions"

for Option #3
❑ large sheets of paper
❑ markers

for Step 5
❑ various Bible translations
❑ chorus book or hymnal
❑ *The Young Messiah* CD (optional)
❑ CD player (optional)

DO:
for Step 2
❑ Duplicate Worksheet 13 "Influenced?"

for Option 2
❑ Enlist a student to do the research and be the "press agent."
❑ Prepare the "press agent" questions on slips of paper

for Step 4
❑ Duplicate Worksheet 14 "A Question of Questions" and fold it on the dotted line.

for Step 5
❑ Select a hymn, chorus, or song.

During the Session

GETTING INVOLVED (10 minutes)
Step 1–Ted or Bill?
Prepare to show the first part of segment seven of *How Now Shall We Live? Student Edition Video*. Explain that Ted and Bill are featured in this segment. As students watch, tell them to decide if they are more like Ted or Bill. After showing the Student Edition Video, ask:
• **In evaluating your overall outlook on life, which are you – Ted, the one who finally asks himself "the hard questions" or Bill, the one who wants a dog? (Invite students to explain their choices.)**
• **If you are like Bill, why have you found it difficult to consider your purpose in life?**
• **If you are like Ted, when did you decide to look for a purpose to your life?**
• **How old will you be in 52 years?**
• **What might you be talking about with your friends from school at your 50th reunion?**
• **What difference do you expect your faith to make in your life over the next 50 years?**
• **Is living a Christian faith something to do when you are older? Why or why not?**

Display the three-question worldview visual used in Unit One. Say: **Tommy (the main character) challenges his friends to ask the hard questions like 'Who am I?' 'What is my purpose in life?' 'How did life get messed**

up?' 'What can I do about it?' Several weeks ago in the early scenes of the video none of these guys cared about the answers to those hard questions.
Ask:
- **What caused Tommy to ask these three worldview questions?**
- **Why do you think Ted followed?**
- **Could you have the same influence on your friends as Tommy had on Ted? (Without the paper bag, of course!) How?**
- **What would it take for your life to influence your friends?**

Explain that during the rest of the session students will evaluate how they are influenced by others and who they influence.

FOCUSING ON THE FACTS (30 minutes)
Step 2—Influenced?
Group students into pairs, with each pair sitting back to back. If possible, spread out. Give one person in each pair a white sheet of paper and a pencil. Hand a copy of Worksheet 13 "Influenced?" to the other person in each pair. Tell each student with a worksheet to describe the abstract drawing to the other person. As the figure is being described, the second student should draw it on the white paper without asking questions. After everyone is finished, compare the drawings.

Say: **All of us have people who influence us. Some give us good messages. Some give us bad messages. Sometimes we get those messages mixed up like some of you did with your drawings. Let's look at who is influencing you and what messages you are getting.**

Hand out paper and pencils to all students. Direct them to record their answers to these three questions:
Question 1. Who has been influential in your life?
These could be people in the past and present. Remind students to list people from the media, in sports, the secular world, from their schools, as well as family members, friends, or religious guides who have influenced them. Tell students to leave space after each name for additional notes.
Question 2. What do you think, believe, or do as a result of knowing each person?
Suggest students make a note or two about specific influences beside the name of each person.
Question 3. Why have you let this person influence you?
This may be a tough question for students to answer honestly. Challenge them to consider why some people are more influential in their lives than others.

As the leader, decide how willing your students will be to share this information. If students have shared openly in past sessions, they should be willing to share

their answers here. Invite volunteers to share first. If students are reluctant, let them get with a friend and share.

As an example of how students may be influenced by others' beliefs, direct them to the three boxes on page 144 of *How Now Shall We Live? Student Edition*. Ask:
- **How many of your friends believe all paths lead to God?**
- **What does it mean that "All truth is God's truth"?**
- **Do either of these beliefs dilute the Christian belief that Jesus is the only way to know God? Why or why not?**

Say: **Martyr was one of the strong Christians you studied this week. Let's look at others.**

Step 3—Spiritually Strong
Direct students to page 147 in the Student Edition. Assign each student or pair of students a verse from the list in the first column. Direct students to look up their assigned verses and decide what power each Scripture offers for today. Call on students to share those examples of power. Tell students to think of specific examples of how that verse might equip a Christian today. In fact, remind students that they may have recorded a story of someone who faced incredible odds and came out with God's victory, on page 147 in the second column. Invite volunteers to share the stories they wrote down.

OPTION 1
If you would like something more creative, hand out construction paper and markers. Tell students that you are creating a new line of greeting cards. You want these new cards to encourage Christians. Assign each verse listed on page 147 in the Student Edition to one or more students. Instruct students to use the verse, or its main thought, in some way in creating their greeting cards. After a few minutes, call on students to share their cards. Continue by letting them share their stories from page 147 as suggested.

OPTION 2
If you have a student who enjoys research, involve that student in looking for more information about St. Patrick, Calvin, or Martyr. Work with the student to prepare five or six questions that the student can answer as a "press agent" for the person who was researched. Write each question on a separate slip of paper and hand these to various students to read. After looking at the examples of power in the Scripture study on page 147, let students ask the questions of the "press agent," instead of telling their stories.

ADDITIONALLY . . . 1
If you have more than an hour for this session, invite students to reflect on how the stories of the people they have studied during these seven weeks have encouraged or helped them. Tell students to look back through their Student Editions and call out the names of Christians who have made a difference in their world. Students may name Jorge Crespo from Unit One, Nicky Cruz from Unit Five, as well as Danny Croce, Justin Martyr, John Calvin, and Patricius from Unit Seven. Ask:
- **How did these people step forward and influence the world around them?**
- **Why were they willing to make a difference?**

MAKING IT REAL (15 minutes)
Step 4—Do I Fit In?
Show Charles Colson's interview on the seventh segment of the Student Edition Video. Direct students to decide why Colson thinks the cultural commission is inseparable from the Great Commission. After playing the video, call for their ideas.

Divide students into teams. Give each team several large sheets of paper, scissors, markers, masking tape, and yarn. Tell each team to dress a person in the cultural influences they see around them. These may be influences from the media, through heroes, in language, family relationships, obedience to authority, school influence, or in other areas of life. The "designer clothes" should reflect these different culture influences. (For example, students could design a hat that symbolizes the cultural idea that greed is good.)

Select one team to dress its model in the redemptive "clothing" of Christianity. Suggest they use phrases from the verses they studied during the week to decorate the Christian clothing. They might also use ideas from Colson's interview.

Call for the fashion show, letting each team share its designer clothing. End with the Christian model. Say: **Cultural influences are very much like clothes. We put on what we want and take it off when we choose. And, just like we want the latest fashion so we won't be out of style, we tend to follow the latest cultural trend.**

OPTION 3
Here's an idea to replace the cultural clothing design activity. Hand out large sheets of paper and markers to groups of students. Tell students to create a listing of "The Top Ten Ways Culture Changes Us." The list can be humorous, but also should be honest. Let different groups share their lists. (Leaders, please notice that next session students will also be asked to create a Top Ten list. That list will be on "The Top Ten Ways Christians Can Change the Culture.")

Hand out pencils and Worksheet 14 "A Question of Questions," folded on the dotted line so students see the top half first. Tell students to complete the top part of the worksheet quickly. Explain that they won't be sharing this information. Next, direct students to unfold the sheet and work through the questions at the bottom. State that they can answer most questions with a yes or no. As students finish the worksheet, say:

A poll by Christian Research, a British organization, determined that of the 1.6 billion Christians in the world, 44 percent said they were "nominal Christians." One of the things that made these people feel "nominal" was that the Church made them uncomfortable because of cultural differences. [1]
Ask:
- **What feelings did you have as you read the questions at the bottom of the sheet?**
- **Do you feel like you need to explain or defend your choices at the top of the sheet, or were you comfortable with your choices?**
- **How does today's culture compromise our Christian faith?**
- **How does today's culture compromise our Christian witness?**
- **What can you learn from this week's study and this session?**

LEAVING PREPARED (5 minutes)
Step 5—Celebrate Jesus!
Say: **Even though you've looked at many negative influences on our culture, we Christians worship a real, living Savior who is greater than all these negatives.**

Either provide a variety of Bible translations or ask students to bring different Bible translations. Request all students turn to *Revelation 5* in the different translations. Call on different ones to read *Revelation 5:12-13* in strong, authoritative voices. Urge each reader to grow more forceful while reading this hymn of praise.

If your students enjoy singing, select a chorus that reflects the words of this praise hymn. "Worthy of Worship" 3, or "Worthy is the Lamb" 157, can be found in *The Baptist Hymnal*. Don Wyrtzen's chorus "Worthy is the Lamb," or Michael W. Smith's "Agnes Dei" are other ideas. Or, you might play "Worthy is the Lamb That Was Slain/Hallelujah" from *The Young Messiah* (Sparrow, 1993). Use this as your closing prayer.

[1] "Who are 'Nominal' Christians?" Youthworker Update, July/August 1999: 10.

Transforming Our Culture

Session Goals
This session is designed to help students:
- examine their personal level of Christian commitment;
- accept the challenge to carry the message of Christ into their culture;
- see practical ways to transform their world.

Session Overview
Step 1: "What's the Big Idea?"—Evaluate the eight weeks of study.

Step 2: The Top Ten—Test ways to change the culture for Christ.

Step 3: It Begins Inside—Understand the need for inner change first.

Step 4: In Summary—Compare the statements of naturalism with the statements of Christianity.

Step 5: Finally. . .—Make a final commitment.

Before the Session

GATHER:
for visual support
- ❑ purpose statement from Introductory Session

for Step 1
- ❑ large banner paper
- ❑ balloons
- ❑ crepe paper streamers
- ❑ markers
- ❑ construction paper cut in half
- ❑ masking tape
- ❑ *How Now Shall We Live? Student Edition Video*
- ❑ TV-VCR
- ❑ pencils
- ❑ Worksheet 15 "A Matter of Salt"

for Step 2
- ❑ poster board or large sheets of paper
- ❑ markers
- ❑ several large boxes

for Option 1
- ❑ large sheets of paper
- ❑ markers

for Step 3
- ❑ Worksheet 16 "What Makes You Salt?"
- ❑ Worksheet 1 "I Believe"

for Option 2
- ❑ white paper
- ❑ envelopes
- ❑ markers

for Step 5
- ❑ small packets of salt

DO:
for Step 1
- ❑ Make the "What the Big Idea?" banner.
- ❑ Decorate the learning environment using the balloons and crepe paper streamers.
- ❑ Duplicate Worksheet 15 "A Matter of Salt."

for Step 2
- ❑ Prepare signs for walls, doors, and boxes.

for Step 3
- ❑ Duplicate Worksheet 16 "What Makes You Salt?" and Worksheet 1 "I Believe."

for Option 2
- ❑ Type out the Bible verses and cut them apart, placing each verse in a separate envelope.

For Step 5
- ❑ Discuss a service project with your pastor or someone connected with a group that needs help.

During the Session

GETTING INVOLVED (10 minutes)
Step 1—"What's the Big Idea?"

Decorate the room to look like the game show on the *How Now Shall We Live? Student Edition Video*. Hang a large banner with "What's the Big Idea?" on it.

Direct each arriving contestant (student) to make a name tag using the construction paper and markers. Tell them to use the word *salt* in their name tags. (For example, one name tag might be John "Salty Dog" Doe.) Attach name tags with masking tape. Let contestants mingle and share their name tags.

Begin by directing attention to the Student Edition Video. Instruct contestants to listen for Tommy's responses for the different religions. Show segment eight. Stop before Colson's interview. After playing the video, call on students to share Tommy's responses. The following gives a synopsis of his comments:

Darwin (evolution)—The missing links are still missing;

Poopsy (utopia)—Sin has been around for 5000 years

and denying sin sounds enlightened, but it's deadly;

Descartes (I think, therefore, I am);—Christians believe God has an absolute, unchanging standard or right and wrong, and I am because God made me;

Naturalism (postmodernity)—a Christian worldview is more consistent, more rational, more workable, it gives me credible answers.

Say: **Eight weeks ago most of us didn't understand what a worldview was. We didn't realize how different belief systems were undermining Christian faith. We didn't think Christians could really make a difference in this out-of-control culture. In this week's final study, you looked at ways Christians make a difference. These people are being salt in their worlds.**

Hand out pencils and copies of Worksheet 15 "A Matter of Salt." (You won't use the bottom portion of this worksheet until Step 5, but leave it attached.) Lead students to repeat *Matthew 5:13-14* as the memory verse. Help students evaluate how they are salty Christians. Ask each to select a type of salt from the worksheet and explain how this type of salt defines who that person is as a Christian. After everyone has shared, ask:
• **In the video why were the salt "people" hesitant to go out into the world?**
• **How do you feel about these hesitant remarks?**

ADDITIONALLY . . . 1

If you have more than an hour for this session, divide contestants into two teams. Tell each team to see which one can be first to answer the "Just the Salt . . ." trivia questions on Worksheet 15 "A Matter of Salt." Use the Bible to confirm the biblical answers. The correct answers are:
1—sodium chloride (give extra points for the knowing the chemical symbol of NaCl)
2—false[1]
3—c *(Num. 18:19)*
4—Sodom, Gomorrah *(Gen. 19:24-26)*
5—Dead Sea
6—Elisha *(2 Kings 2:20-21)*
7—true[2]

FOCUSING ON THE FACTS (30 minutes)
Step 2—The Top Ten
Continue with the game show motif. Before the session, prepare posters or signs by writing each of the following on separate posters using large letters:

Officer Sal, "broken window" theory, zero tolerance, the "Mrs. Greene" syndrome, tranquillitas ordinis, Jencks' idea, Larson's psychiatry.

Hang posters facing the wall. Hang door signs so students must open a door to see the sign. Place other signs in large boxes. Direct contestants to select a box, a door, or a poster. (If you have more than seven students, let them work in pairs or small teams.) Tell contestants to

reveal their topics and research the one assigned to them using the ideas in Unit Eight of *How Now Shall We Live? Student Edition*. Direct contestants to present their research in an informative, game show fashion. For example, they could make it a quiz ("Is that your final answer?") or have choices like "Let's Make a Deal" or use key words like "Password." Encourage contestants to share if any of these ideas or theories have been used in their schools or communities (for example, zero tolerance).

After ideas and theories are presented, say: **In the Student Edition you read about several Christians who are changing the cultures where they are. You also read Colson's statement that, "No worldview is merely theoretical philosophy; worldview is intensely practical." Let's get practical.** (p. 172)

Invite contestants to work in pairs or small teams. Hand each a large sheet of paper and a marker. Direct them to list the "Top Ten Ways Christians Can Change the Culture." This culture may involve their school campus, their neighborhood, their city, their circle of friends, or wherever they view as the boundaries of their culture. Although these can be humorous, urge contestants to also be practical. Display contestants' lists to use later. If students think of additional ways, add these to the lists.

OPTION 1

Instead of making "Top Ten" lists, plan a debate with a twist. Debate the statement: Christians are responsible for social reform. Assign one team to support the statement and the other team to refute the statement. Give both teams large sheets of paper and markers. Tell each team to make its points by offering suggestions of specific things Christians can do. For example, the side supporting the statement should list specific ways Christians can be involved in social reforms. The side refuting the statement should list specific ways Christians can live out their worldviews without supporting social reform. Display the large sheets of paper as each side makes it points. Allow time for teams to offer rebuttal statements. You can continue the game show theme during the debate.

Step 3—It Begins Inside
Say: **So far, we've looked at how Christians in general, also known as "the church," can make a difference in their culture. On Day Four you examined how redeeming a culture begins from the inside out. Too many Christians think they need to change the world, but fail to let their souls and their lives be changed.**

Hand out copies of Worksheet 16 "What Makes You Salt?" Suggest students take a few moments to review the verses and select three or four to rewrite from a personal point of view. Encourage them to add their own favorite verses. Before students share, invite them to repeat the memory verse, *Matthew 5:13-14*. Ask: **What makes you salt?** as each student shares one or two verses.

OPTION 2

Younger students may not be as reflective as older students. Type out each Scripture from the worksheet in large words. Cut the verse(s) into phrases of three or four words. Put each verse in a separate envelope. Write the biblical reference on the envelope. Hand out the envelopes, telling contestants to put together the verses within a certain time limit. Let them check their accuracy by looking up the verse in the Bible. Next, direct contestants to use a marker to write a paraphrase of the verse using the backs of the strips of paper. Let contestants put these slips back in the envelopes and swap the envelopes with others. Each person then has to put together the paraphrased thought. Call on each person to read the original thought from the Bible (using the Scripture reference on the envelope) and the paraphrased version.

Remind students of the "I Believe" worksheet they completed in the Introductory Session. Hand out copies of Worksheet 1 "I Believe." Tell students to quickly check their beliefs. Ask:
• **After eight weeks do you recognize any statements where you might have changed as a result of this study?** (Invite students to share those that might have changed.)
• **With which statements do you still agree?**
• **With which statements do you disagree?** (Encourage students to support their ideas.)

Point out that many of the statements come from this last unit. Here are reference pages for students who are interested in discussing the statements: 1 p. 140; 2 p. 166; 3 no page; 4 pp. 137, 165; 5 p. 111; 6 no page; 7 p. 139; 8 p. 170; 9 p. 137; 10 p. 171. Encourage students to review their worldview statements written in the front of the Student Edition. Ask them how these statements may have changed during the study.

MAKING IT REAL (10 minutes)
Step 4—In Summary
Remind students that they read two paragraphs on Day Four that summarized the study of *How Now Shall We Live?* Direct students to page 168 in the Student Edition. Tell one person to read the paragraph that begins, "In a nutshell..." saying the number before each statement which person identified as a summarizing statement. Ask a second person to read the paragraph that begins, "By contrast, . . .," also reading the numbers that person inserted before each biblical plan statement. Tell one

student to read one statement, then the other student read the opposite statement, back and forth until all statements are read. Urge students to listen for the great differences between the two worldviews.

Say: **Some people don't accept the Bible as proof of Christianity. Others don't understand the words or phrases Christians often use. For example, a friend may not know what salvation means or even who Jesus is other than a cuss word.**
    Ask:
• **How can you share your faith with your culture?**
• **How can you express your worldview in terms others understand?**

Display the purpose statement visual from the Introductory Session. If students changed this statement in the Unit One, display the revised purpose.
    Ask:
• **Did we achieve our purpose? Why or why not?**
• **What happens next?**

OPTION 3

Replace the summary statements activity by challenging students to write a *Help Wanted* ad for the newspaper or a website. The ad should be seeking "salt," however students choose to interpret that one word after today's study. Leaders, be prepared. Younger students take things literally and may write an ad for sodium chloride! Call on volunteers to share their advertisements.

LEAVING PREPARED (10 minutes)
Step 5—Finally . . .
Play the final segment of the Student Edition Video with Charles Colson. As the video ends, hand out small packets of salt. Point out the two incomplete statements at the bottom of Worksheet 15 "A Matter of Salt" handed out in Step 1. Using the "Top Ten" lists from Step 2, encourage students to record one way they can be salt in their world. Suggest they choose something they can do immediately, or may already be doing. For the second incomplete statement, point out that the job of the church is to equip Christians to go out. Lead students to commit to a plan to transform their culture as a group, too. If possible, make specific plans. Let your pastor or someone from a missions committee suggest places where the group can work together. Suggest students write down both commitments on their worksheets.

    Direct students to place the small salt packets in their Bibles to mark *Matthew 5:13-14*. Lead students in saying these two verses a final time. Invite students to pray about their commitments as salt and light.

[1] Gunther Salt Company, <http://www.gunthersalt.com/gs_trivia.htm> 1 Feb. 2000.
[2] Ibid.

I Believe

Agree or disagree with each of the following statements.

I Believe

Agree	Disagree	
❏	❏	1. There are two basic laws in life—scientific law which deals with facts and truths and moral law which deals with values and religion.
❏	❏	2. The Holy Spirit can reveal new truth that might contradict what the Bible says.
❏	❏	3. I will have time later as a Christian to live a decent, moral life.
❏	❏	4. What I do in my private life is my business.
❏	❏	5. Human beings can reach inside themselves to find a guide for life.
❏	❏	6. I am a sinner, saved by God through my belief in Jesus Christ.
❏	❏	7. Salvation is merely freedom from sin.
❏	❏	8. Knowing God makes people happier and healthier.
❏	❏	9. My faith is a very personal matter between me and God.
❏	❏	10. All religion is beneficial.

Tell the Truth

Card 1–I am Professor Anne Arkist–a scientist and a zoologist. In fact, I am President of the International Society for People With More Brains Than They Need–oh, yes, and the mother of two. I believe that evil is merely bad behavior resulting from the repressive, closed-minded, male dominated, Judeo-Christian culture.

Card 2–I am a renowned psychologist from Kahuna Luna's Center for Meditative Oneness in Laguna Beach. I've written over a half-dozen pamphlets on living with bad karma. I enjoy surfing and barnacle harvesting. You can call me Monty. I believe that truth cannot be defined or measured, but is real only if I think it is real.

Card 3–I am a salesman with a answer for every possible question you might have. I can guarantee that my answers will calm every teenage anxiety, fill every student's heart, and soothe every youthful problem. No more wondering about where you came from or why you're here. My product–Naturalism–says "Build your own life! Forget about an afterlife. Who needs it? You've got today, so make the most of it."

How Now Shall We Live? Student Edition Leader's Guide

3 1

Concentration Game

Important: Duplicate worksheets 3A (front) and 3B (back) before cutting apart the cards.

1	2
3	4
5	6
7	8
9	10
11	12
13	14
15	16
17	18
19	20

Worksheet 3B (Back Side)

Important: Duplicate worksheets 3A (front) and 3B (back) before cutting apart the cards.

theism	the most general beliefs, concepts, and attitudes of an individual or group
the belief that whatever works best is right	utopianism
the belief that in life there is no right or wrong	deconstructionism
the belief that scientific laws are adequate for all phenomena; denies that any event or object can have supernatural significance	the call to create a culture under the lordship of Christ
the belief that the right social and economic structures will create an age of harmony and prosperity	philosophy
the belief that does away with private property through a system in which goods are owned in common and are available to all as needed	enlightenment
communism	cultural commission
postmodernism	postmodern belief that law is based on the opinion of whoever is in power at the time
naturalism	pragmatism
the belief in God	movement that rejected traditional social, religious, and political ideas to emphasize that reasoning decides right from wrong

Research Sites

E X A M I N E   T H E
𝕰𝖛𝖎𝖉𝖊𝖓𝖈𝖊 𝖔𝖋 𝕯𝖎𝖛𝖎𝖓𝖊 𝕮𝖗𝖊𝖆𝖙𝖎𝖔𝖓
AND PRESENT THAT EVIDENCE IN CLEAR, UNDERSTANDABLE FORM. YOU MAY:

(1) present your evidence as a prosecutor at a trial;
(2) prepare a skit featuring those who present false evidence and someone who corrects them;
(3) write a rap or develop a choral reading using sign language.

Evidence of a Divine Creator or by Chance? (Day 1)

By Chance—Main Evidence
·
·
·

Divine Creation—Biblical Evidence
• *Psalm 139:13-16*
• *1 Corinthians 2:9-10*

Evidence of a Divine Creator or by Change? (Day 2)

By Change—Main Evidence
·
·
·

Divine Creation—Biblical Evidence
• *Genesis 1:11-12, 21, 24-25*
• *Colossians 1:16-17*

Evidence of a Divine Creator or by Natural Forces? (Day 3)

By Natural Forces—Main Evidence
·
·
·

Divine Creation—Biblical Evidence
• *Job 38:33*
• *Isaiah 40:13-14*

Evidence of a Divine Creator by a Big Bang? (Day 4)

By a Big Bang—Main Evidence
·
·
·

Divine Creation—Biblical Evidence
• *Genesis 1:3*
• *Job 38:4-11*
• *Hebrews 11:3*

Evidence of a Divine Creator by Design? (Day 5)

By Design—Main Evidence
·
·
·

Divine Creation—Biblical Evidence
• Job 37:5
• Isaiah 40:28
• John 1:1

We've Got Questions

As you watch *How Now Shall We Live? Student Edition Video*, look for this information.

1. Who asks, "Who put the bang in the Big Bang?"

2. Where did Tommy go after asking this question, "Can you tell me that life is more than a random set of occurrences, determined by mutations and genetic codes with no true meaning, but what I choose to ascribe to it in this particular moment along the time space continuum?"

3. When Tommy and Darwin talk, Tommy asks, "Why don't you give it up?!" What does Darwin see as the alternate if he gives up his evolution theory?

4. What makes Tommy mad at Darwin?

5. What does Tommy think about Darwin's final comments?

- -

Worksheet 5B
Doxology

"Is there anyone around who can explain God?
Anyone smart enough to tell him what to do?
Anyone who has done him such a huge favor
that God has to ask his advice?"

Everything comes from him:
Everything happens through him;
Everything ends up in him.
Always glory! Always praise!
Yes. Yes. Yes.
Amen
Romans 11:33-36

Eugene H. Peterson, *The Message* (Colorado Springs, CO: NavPress, 1995).

Statements of Worldviews

1. The Cosmos is all that is, or ever was, or ever will be.

2. In every human being is a deep, ongoing search for meaning.

3. The fear of the Lord is the beginning of wisdom.

4. We are made to worship.

5. Morality is not based on personal feelings, but on the way human nature was created.

6. We see the world through the perspective of race, gender, and ethnic group.

7. Someone or something other than me causes me to do wrong.

8. We must acknowledge a standard outside ourselves and be accountable for sin.

9. Men do not make the laws; they merely discover them.

10. Nothing working on nothing by nothing, through nothing, for nothing, begat everything.

11. Only love changes human behavior.

12. Truth is a tool to help us get what we want.

13. The logic of the human mind is the source of certainty.

14. We are guided by our own instincts; we do not chose what we will do.

15. I am the Alpha and the Omega, . . . who is, and who was, and who is to come.

Gotta Believe Check-up

Read each statement. If you accept the statement as true, place a mark in the first box. Your leader will tell you what to do with the second set of boxes.

True

1. Every human being has a natural desire to do wrong. ❏ ❏

2. If education were improved, people could earn more money and crime would stop. ❏ ❏

3. The problems in my life right now are not my fault, but are caused by
   forces beyond my control. ❏ ❏

4. The best way to get rid of a corrupting influence is to eliminate it. ❏ ❏

5. The main reasons for violence among today's students are Internet
   addiction and dysfunctional families. ❏ ❏

6. The devil is the cause of sin in today's world. ❏ ❏

7. Sin is not my problem; it's God's. ❏ ❏

8. No child starts out to be bad; he or she has to be taught. ❏ ❏

9. People are complex animals who operate on uncontrollable impulses. ❏ ❏

10. The church really creates evil by making people to feel guilty. ❏ ❏

11. The seven deadly sins (lust, greed, pride, anger, envy, laziness, and gluttony)
    are not evils, but rather human compulsions or addictions. ❏ ❏

12. The world is actually getting better, not worse. ❏ ❏

The Campaign Trail

Candidate Name

Platform: The Problem With the World Today Is . . .

Candidate's Position on Sin:

Scripture to Consult:

Romans 3:10-20; 7:7

Romans 5:12-21

Romans 6:11-19

Campaign Emphasis
(Use these points to develop the elements of your campaign, including a campaign slogan, song, 30-second commercial, and brief platform speech for the candidate.)

*

*

*

*

Campaign Slogan

Campaign Song

Campaign Commercial

Platform Notes

Cards and Questions

George Friedrich Hegel	Laid groundwork for communist movement; his goal was a classless society.
Karl Marx	Saw human nature as naturally loving and good; society caused oppression and corruption.
Jean-Jacques Rousseau	Believed people are controlled by their animal impulses; father of psychoanalysis.
Sigmund Freud	Crusader for birth control and sexual liberation to save our bodies from stunting potential.
Margaret Sanger	Saw sexuality as a means to salvation; reduced sex to biological act of orgasm.
Alfred Kinsey	Believed humans must release universal energy through sexual activity.
Wilhelm Reich	Saw progress as inevitable, moving towards perfection through human effort.

Person's Name: _____

1. Where did we come from?

2. What has gone wrong with the world?

3. What can we do to fix it?

Worksheet 10
Duh?!

Think of your friends. Probably some of them are Christians who may not realize how their thoughts are being shaped by others. You also may have friends who are not Christians.

This session deals with several different ideas. How would you explain these ideas taken from segment 5 of the How Now Shall We Live? Student Edition Video to your friends? Make notes on this worksheet about what you might say to both your Christian friends and your non-Christian friends concerning these ideas.

TOMMY: Do you think that all human beings yearn, deep in their hearts, for deliverance from sin and guilt, for freedom and meaning? Do you think we try to suppress the longing, to rationalize it away, to mute it with lesser answers? But, ultimately it's impossible to evade. Sooner or later, even the most decent among us knows that there is rottenness at our core.

BARK: Thomas, you need to see the universe as the product of constant change . . . Evolution. Each day we move farther from our primitive beginning and closer to a glorious future. History is a dynamic series of step as human ingenuity moves us from one level to the next—an endless progression toward perfection.

MARX: *Religion is the illusory sun around which man revolves, until he begins to revolve around himself. That is my goal—to be independent—to stand on my own two feet; and I only stand on my own feet when I owe my existence to myself alone.*

TOMMY: You think ideas don't have consequences? You tell people that pushing our way to the next stage of evolution is the goal. So they tear down everything around them! And anyone who might see things differently is exterminated like a cockroach in the cupboard. You deny the evil in human nature, so your followers place no checks and balances on personal power, and we all know what absolute power does . . . Right?
   It corrupts absolutely! Don't you guys read history? World views have consequences! Especially when they're wrong!

God is…

Complete the missing idea with a word or phrase that expresses how that belief system would finish the statement. Use the material you studied this week in Unit Six.

	science	genetics	extraterrestrials	existentialism	New Age	Christianity
God is . . .						
Sin is . . .						
I am . . .						
Salvation comes from . . .						
Truth is found in . . .						
Look for hope in . . .						
The way to relate to others is . . .						

Would You Rather? Cards

Cut these cards apart so each student can have one card.

Would you rather have hope or wealth?	Would you rather see or not see the point to life?
Would you rather morality be based on opinion or truth?	Would you rather understand the universe or the opposite sex?
Would you rather build a life on knowledge or faith?	Would you rather know there is life on other planets or know there is no life on other planets?
Would your rather trust a person or a supernatural being?	Would you rather know there was life after death or know that life ended with death?
Would you rather talk about something you've experienced or something you've read about?	Would you rather be known for your loyalty or your integrity?
Would you rather know things in life were getting better or worse?	Would you rather die for a lie or die for the truth?

Influenced?

A Question of Questions

[a single sheet to be folded by the leader]

1. Write the name of your favorite song or recording artist.

2. What was the last movie you saw?

3. What TV program do you watch regularly?

4. What words or phrases do you say when you are surprised, angry, or extremely excited?

5. Name the website you visit most frequently.

6. What topic do you often discuss with your friends?

- -

The thief comes only to steal and kill and destroy; I have come that they may have life, and have it to the full." John 10:10

Have you participated in any activity that might compromise or destroy your Christian faith or witness?

Have you participated in any activity that might help you live up to Jesus' desire for your life?

The weapons we fight with are not the weapons of the world . . . We take captive every thought to make it obedient to Christ. 2 Corinthians 10:4-5

Have you exposed yourself to explicit material that pollutes your thoughts?

Then, you will know the truth, and the truth will set you free." John 8:32

Do you spend the same amount of time with the truth (Bible study, prayer, Christian fellowship) as you do with other activities?

You belong to your father, the devil, and you want to carry out your father's desire . . . When he lies, he speaks his native language, for he is a liar and the father of lies." John 8:44

Are you lying to yourself about what you see or do or say?

Let us fix our eyes on Jesus, the author and perfecter of our faith . . .Consider him who endured such opposition from sinful men, so that you will not grow weary, and lose heart." Hebrews 12:2-3

Do your words and actions reflect your understanding of the price Jesus Christ paid for you?

A Matter of Salt

Which kind of "salt" are you as a Christian? Be prepared to share why.

I am like . . .

❑ rock salt (to melt ice in making ice cream or on icy sidewalks)
❑ salt tablets (to replace salt in the body)
❑ salt bricks or licks (for animals)
❑ pretzel salt
❑ iodized salt (table, cooking salt)
❑ solar salt (used in conditioning water)

because . . .

Just the Salt . . .

1. The chemical name for salt is _____.

2. True or False. Salt dissolves more quickly in hot water rather than cold.

3. In Old Testament times salt was used in legalizing (a) marriages; (b) property sales; (c) covenants; (d) all of the above.

4. Lot's wife turned into a pillar of salt after looking back at the destruction of _____ and _____.

5. The Salt Sea of Israel is also known as the _____.

6. (a) Elijah; (b) Elisha; (c) Jeremiah; or (d) Jesus threw salt into a stagnant pool to make it pure.

7. True or false. The word salary comes from the idea of salt being used in payment for a person's services.

I will be salt

We will be salt

What Makes You Salt?

"You are the salt of the earth. But if the salt loses its saltiness, how can it be made salty again? It is no longer good for anything, except to be thrown out and trampled by men. You are the light of the world. A city on a hill cannot be hidden." (Matthew 5:13-14)

You bring your own gifts, abilities, and experiences to your Christian worldview. The biblical truths in these verses are for every Christian. Select several verses to put into your own words. How does that verse fit into your life? How does it make you salt?

Psalm 85:8

Isaiah 1:17

Matthew 15:17-19

Matthew 22:37-40

1 Corinthians 10:23

Ephesians 4:28

1 Thessalonians 4:11-12

James 1:22

James 1:27

1 Peter 5:8

Add your favorite verse here:

Treasure Hunt

What are the three parts of a worldview? page 13

Who was Descartes? page 22

Who was Rousseau? page 23

Who was Darwin? page 24

What is DNA? page 41

What is the Big Bang? page 45

Who was Sagan and what was his trademark phrase? page 55

What is relativism? pages 65, 68

What is "The Fall?" page 74

What was Marx's mistake? page 81, 95

What is the utopian view? page 75

Who was Freud? page 83

What is the escalator fallacy? page 93

Who was Sanger? page 101

Who was Kinsey? page 102

What are Comte's stages of social evolution? page 113

What are Muller's stages of genetic evolution? page 114

What are the weaknesses of the New Age? page 127

Who was Sarte? page 119

What is the cultural mandate? page 138

Who was Justin Martyr? page 143

Who was Patrick the missionary? page 145

What does shalom really mean? page 159

What is the "Mrs. Greene Syndrome"? page 162